James Augustine Aloysius Joyce was born in Dublin in 1882 and educated at Jesuit schools and University College, Dublin, where he studied philosophy and languages. In 1900, while he was still an undergraduate, his long review of Ibsen's last play was published in *Fortnightly Review*. At this time he also began to write the lyric poems later collected in *Chamber Music*.

In 1902 Joyce left Dublin for Paris, but returned the following year as his mother was dying. From 1904 he lived with Nora Barnacle; they were eventually married in 1931. Their home from 1905 to 1915 was Trieste, where Joyce taught English at the Berlitz School. In 1909 and 1912 he made his last trips to Ireland, attempting to arrange publication of *Dubliners* which finally appeared in England in 1914.

During 1915 Joyce wrote his one published play, *Exiles*. *A Portrait of the Artist as a Young Man* appeared in 1916. In the same year Joyce and his family moved to Zürich where they lived in great poverty while Joyce worked on *Ulysses*, which first appeared in serial form in the American magazine, *The Little Review*. Serialization began in 1918 but was suspended in 1920 following prosecution. *Ulysses* was published in book form in 1922 in Paris, where the Joyce family remained during the interwar years. In 1939 *Finnegan's Wake* was published and in 1940 the Joyces returned to Switzerland. Two months later, in January 1941, James Joyce died. *Stephen Hero*, part of the first draft of *Portrait*, was posthumously published in 1944.

Also by James Joyce

James Joyce

Exiles

A Play in Three Acts

With the author's own notes
and an introduction by
Padraic Colum

A TRIAD PANTHER BOOK

GRANADA PUBLISHING
London Toronto Sydney New York

Published by Granada Publishing Limited
in Panther Books 1979

ISBN 0 586 04806 5

First published in 1918
First published in Great Britain by
Jonathan Cape 1921

Granada Publishing Limited
Frogmore, St Albans, Herts AL2 2NF
and
3 Upper James Street, London W1R 4BP
1221 Avenue of the Americas, New York, NY 10020, USA
117 York Street, Sydney, NSW 2000, Australia
100 Skyway Avenue, Toronto, Ontario, Canada M9W 3A6
110 Northpark Centre, 2193 Johannesburg, South Africa
CML Centre, Queen & Wyndham, Auckland 1, New Zealand

Set, printed and bound in Great Britain by
Cox & Wyman Ltd.,
London, Reading and Fakenham
Set in Linotype Juliana

Contents

The Notes which follow the play were written by Mr Joyce in a blue-covered blankbook which is now the property of the University of Buffalo. The publishers acknowledge the gracious co-operation of that institution and of Mr Charles D. Abbott, its Director of Libraries, as well as of the administrators of the estate of James Joyce

Introduction

To break deliberately with an order one has been brought up in, a social, moral and spiritual order, and, out of one's own convictions, to endeavour to create a new order, is to embark on a lonely and hazardous enterprise. Stephen Daedalus at the end of A *Portrait of the Artist as a Young Man* contemplates doing this. Richard Rowan in *Exiles* has attempted it. Through secrecy and exile Stephen Daedalus would forge the uncreated conscience of his race. He would go into his exile alone. Richard Rowan, going into exile, brought Bertha with him, and on two he left behind, Beatrice Justice and Robert Hand, he left the impress of his personality. The struggle on Richard Rowan's side to free friendship and love from all their bonds makes the drama of *Exiles*.

Exiles is not a play about adultery, actual or suspected; the writer of A *Portrait of the Artist* is not going to lay before us anything so banal; it is not a duel between Richard Rowan and Robert Hand for the possession of Bertha. In the crucial scene one says to the other, 'A battle of both our souls, different as they are, against all that is false in them and in the world. A battle of your soul against the spectre of fidelity, of mine against the spectre of friendship.'

What has this to do with exile as a theme? The title of the play is no misnomer, although Richard Rowan is now back in his native city and is being received as well as might be expected. For Bertha, Beatrice Justice, Robert Hand have been taken, as Richard Rowan took himself, beyond the accepted moralities and to where they have to make choices for themselves.

Among Joyce's works his single play has never been given a fair show. *Exiles* comes after *Portrait of the Artist* and before *Ulysses*, and critics have recorded their feeling that it has not the enchantment of the first nor the richness of the second, and they have neglected to assess what quality it actually has. They have noted that *Exiles* has the shape of an Ibsen play and have discounted it as being the derivative work of a young admirer of the great Scandinavian dramatist. It has certain characteristics that suggest one of the later Ibsen plays. With clearly defined form it has spareness and significance of dialogue. And at an important part it has an accidental resemblance to a well-known scene in an Ibsen play: when Robert Hand enters there is much about him to recall Judge Brack. And this resemblance, besides giving a sense of something reminiscent, also gives a wrong lead. But it should be noted that the attempt to set up a three-cornered establishment has no effect in Joyce's play. And in *Exiles* the situations, being motivated by a Catholic and not a Protestant conscience, are different from the situations in an Ibsen play.

As he was working on it, Joyce made copious notes for *Exiles*, notes that were directives for himself and which are being published with the present edition. The copy-book in which the notes were written was saved from Mr Joyce's apartment, 17 rue des Vignes, Paris, in 1940 by his confidant, Paul L. Léon, who consigned it with other documents to the care of a friend who, in April 1948, restored all of the material to Mr Léon's widow.

In some of the notes there is a strain of youthfulness. There is youthfulness in the notion that, as the Scandinavian heroines of Ibsen have supplanted the Slav heroines of the Russian novelists, it may be that a Celtic heroine, his own Bertha, will supplant the Scandinavian. There is youthfulness, too, in the affinity he sees between Bertha and Isolde. In reading these notes – they have the revelation of a long soliloquy – we perceive that *Exiles* is a sort of watershed between the work James Joyce has done and the work he is to do. There is a comparison of Bertha with the earth made in the notes, a comparison that suggests she is facing toward Mollie Bloom. She is seen as the moon, too. In the play she is living near the beach on which Ulysses-Bloom is to see Nausicaa-Gertie. She has in her the virginal Gertie MacDowell. And there is a passage in the notes that lets us know that Joyce will treat his Bertha as Mollie Bloom: a modern writer, he tells us, Paul de Kock, writes a hesitating, painful story about cuckoldry, while his forefathers, Rabelais and Molière, were able to get salacity and humour into their accounts of the subject. He will go back to Rabelais and Molière.

If James Joyce had gone from *Portrait of the Artist* to *Ulysses* (and according to the way most commentators discount *Exiles* he might as well have done this) we should not have known the drama that was implicit in Stephen Daedalus's resolve to forge the uncreated conscience of his race. The drama is poignant in *Exiles*. And we should not have known that Joyce was able to give an appealing presentation of a young woman. Bertha, it is true, is a development of Gretta, Gabriel Conroy's wife, in 'The Dead'. Gretta exists only through her grief for the young man who lies under the nettles in Rahoon. But Bertha exists through her tenderness, her pride, her capability of sorrow for a past, which is also the sorrow of exile, and her resentments which come out of her awareness of her own simplicity. She is a woman who can weep and with whose tears we can sympathize because they are for things that are irretrievably lost – an unspoiled youthful love. She is not really concerned with principles, and she looks on philosophical discourse as a game that engages men's wandering minds. She is neither shocked nor thrilled at Richard's break with the order she was brought up in and his dedication to the creation of a new order. Being a woman, she has in herself an immemorial and universal order.

It is the woman who cannot give anything freely, Beatrice Justice, who can understand Richard Rowan's mind, and she can understand it because it has a repressed part of herself, her pride and her scorn. Richard's exile has divided her life into halves. She has recovered from an illness that was the consequence of his departure, but her life will be the life of a convalescent. As a Protestant she is not dismayed by Richard Rowan's attempt to transvalue the values of his people. He had initiated a correspondence with her and had kept it up for nine years, and Bertha, lonely in her exile, had meditated on the person he gave so much of his mind to. She meets her and is jealous – not jealous, perhaps, but envious – of an intelligence and education that can attract Richard; then she loses her grievance and becomes friendly with her. And now

9

it should be possible for Richard Rowan to retain Beatrice Justice as a devoted friend. Richard may have wanted that. But his probings at the beginning of the play were directed to showing her that she is in love with him and so making it impossible for one with her kind of conscience to stay near him. Then Beatrice fades out of the play.

His relation with Beatrice Justice shows Richard Rowan as a moralist, and a narrow moralist at that. Not his gay father but his austere mother is the one he would bring into his life. It is Robert Hand who is the immoralist in *Exiles* – but only conventionally an immoralist. He is able to offer Bertha simplicities for Richard's subtleties. He might be one of the students Stephen Daedalus left behind when he chose secrecy and exile as a means of forging the uncreated conscience of his race, one of the students who, mature now, has found his place in the world. And yet he says something that makes him extraordinary. 'A battle of your soul against the spectre of fidelity, of mine against the spectre of friendship. All life is conquest, the victory of human passion over the commandment of cowardice.' Yes, but Beatrice Justice had seen that her cousin had become a pale reflection of another. Is this a challenge from himself or from that part of him that imagines Richard Rowan? Richard knows him as a disciple who will betray his master. For Richard Rowan the struggle between them eventuates in the breaking of bonds, the bond between master and disciple, the bond of his security in his love for Bertha. In the end, the order that Bertha maintained in herself is shown to be more fundamental than the order Richard would destroy or the order he would create. It is Richard Rowan's sense of fatherhood and Bertha's tenderness for her man that are left as the means by which the transvaluer of accepted values will be healed of his self-inflicted wound. In its structure, *Exiles* is a series of confessions; the dialogue has the dryness of recitals in the confessional; its end is an act of contrition.

PADRAIC COLUM

EXILES

A Play in Three Acts

Characters

RICHARD ROWAN, a writer.
BERTHA.
ARCHIE, their son, aged eight years.
ROBERT HAND, journalist.
BEATRICE JUSTICE, his cousin, music teacher.
BRIGID, an old servant of the Rowan family.
A FISHERWOMAN.

At Merrion and Ranelagh, suburbs of Dublin.
Summer of the year 1912.

FIRST ACT

The drawingroom in Richard Rowan's house at Merrion, a suburb of Dublin. On the right, forward, a fireplace, before which stands a low screen. Over the mantelpiece a giltframed glass. Further back in the right wall, folding doors leading to the parlour and kitchen. In the wall at the back to the right a small door leading to a study. Left of this a sideboard. On the wall above the sideboard a framed crayon drawing of a young man. More to the left double doors with glass panels leading out to the garden. In the wall at the left a window looking out on the road. Forward in the same wall a door leading to the hall and the upper part of the house. Between the window and door a lady's davenport stands against the wall. Near it a wicker chair. In the centre of the room a round table. Chairs, upholstered in faded green plush, stand round the table. To the right, forward, a smaller table with a smoking service on it. Near it an easychair and a lounge. Cocoanut mats lie before the fireplace, beside the lounge and before the doors. The floor is of stained planking. The double doors at the back and the folding doors at the right have lace curtains, which are drawn halfway. The lower sash of the window is lifted and the window is hung with heavy green plush curtains. The blind is pulled down to the edge of the lifted lower sash. It is a warm afternoon in June and the room is filled with soft sunlight which is waning.

[BRIGID and BEATRICE JUSTICE come in by the door on the left. BRIGID is an elderly woman, lowsized, with irongrey hair. BEATRICE JUSTICE is a slender dark young woman of 27 years. She wears a wellmade navyblue costume and an elegant simply trimmed black straw hat, and carries a small portfolioshaped handbag.]

BRIGID

The mistress and Master Archie is at the bath. They never expected you. Did you send word you were back, Miss Justice?

13

No. I arrived just now.

BRIGID

[*Points to the easychair.*] Sit down and I'll tell the master you are here. Were you long in the train?

BEATRICE

[*Sitting down.*] Since morning.

BRIGID

Master Archie got your postcard with the views of Youghal. You're tired out, I'm sure.

BEATRICE

O no. [*She coughs rather nervously.*] Did he practise the piano while I was away?

BRIGID

[*Laughs heartily.*] Practise, how are you! Is it Master Archie? He is mad after the milkman's horse now. Had you nice weather down there, Miss Justice?

BEATRICE

Rather wet. I think.

BRIGID

[*Sympathetically.*] Look at that now. And there is rain over-head too. [*Moving towards the study.*] I'll tell him you are here.

BEATRICE

Is Mr Rowan in?

BRIGID

[*Points.*] He is in his study. He is wearing himself out about something he is writing. Up half the night he does be. [*Going.*] I'll call him.

BEATRICE

Don't disturb him, Brigid. I can wait here till they come back if they are not long.

BRIGID

And I saw something in the letterbox when I was letting you

in. [*She crosses to the study door, opens it slightly and calls.*]
Master Richard, Miss Justice is here for Master Archie's
lesson.

[RICHARD ROWAN *comes in from the study and advances
towards* BEATRICE, *holding out his hand. He is a tall
athletic young man of a rather lazy carriage. He has
light brown hair and a moustache and wears glasses. He
is dressed in loose lightgrey tweed.*]

RICHARD

Welcome.

BEATRICE

[*Rises and shakes hands, blushing slightly.*] Good afternoon,
Mr Rowan. I did not want Brigid to disturb you.

RICHARD

Disturb me? My goodness!

BRIGID

There is something in the letterbox, sir.

RICHARD

[*Takes a small bunch of keys from his pocket and hands them
to her.*] Here.

[BRIGID *goes out by the door at the left and is heard
opening and closing the box. A short pause. She enters
with two newspapers in her hands.*]

RICHARD

Letters?

BRIGID

No, sir. Only them Italian newspapers.

RICHARD

Leave them on my desk will you?

[BRIGID *hands him back the keys, leaves the newspapers
in the study, comes out again and goes out by the folding doors on the right.*]

RICHARD

Please, sit down. Bertha will be back in a moment.

[BEATRICE *sits down again in the easychair.* RICHARD *sits beside the table.*]

RICHARD

I had begun to think you would never come back. It is twelve days since you were here.

BEATRICE

I thought of that too. But I have come.

RICHARD

Have you thought over what I told you when you were here last?

BEATRICE

Very much.

RICHARD

You must have known it before. Did you? [*She does not answer.*] Do you blame me?

BEATRICE

No.

RICHARD

Do you think I have acted towards you – badly? No? Or towards anyone?

BEATRICE

[*Looks at him with a sad puzzled expression.*] I have asked myself that question.

RICHARD

And the answer?

BEATRICE

I could not answer it.

RICHARD

If I were a painter and told you I had a book of sketches of you you would not think it so strange, would you?

BEATRICE

It is not quite the same case, is it?

RICHARD

[*Smiles slightly.*] Not quite. I told you also that I would not show you what I had written unless you asked to see it. Well?

16

BEATRICE

I will not ask you.

RICHARD

[*Leans forward, resting his elbows on his knees, his hands joined.*] Would you like to see it?

BEATRICE

Very much.

RICHARD

Because it is about yourself?

BEATRICE

Yes. But not only that.

RICHARD

Because it is written by me? Yes? Even if what you would find there is sometimes cruel?

BEATRICE

[*Shyly.*] That is part of your mind, too.

RICHARD

Then it is my mind that attracts you? Is that it?

BEATRICE

[*Hesitating, glances at him for an instant.*] Why do you think I come here?

RICHARD

Why? Many reasons. To give Archie lessons. We have known one another so many years, from childhood, Robert, you and I – haven't we? You have always been interested in me, before I went away and while I was away. Then our letters to each other about my book. Now it is published. I am here again. Perhaps you feel that some new thing is gathering in my brain; perhaps you feel that you should know it. Is that the reason?

BEATRICE

No.

RICHARD

Why, then?

BEATRICE

Otherwise I could not see you.

[*She looks at him for a moment and then turns aside quickly.*]

RICHARD

[*After a pause repeats uncertainly.*] Otherwise you could not see me?

BEATRICE

[*Suddenly confused.*] I had better go. They are not coming back. [*Rising.*] Mr Rowan, I must go.

RICHARD

[*Extending his arms.*] But you are running away. Remain. Tell me what your words mean. Are you afraid of me?

BEATRICE

[*Sinks back again.*] Afraid? No.

RICHARD

Have you confidence in me? Do you feel that you know me?

BEATRICE

[*Again shyly.*] It is hard to know anyone but oneself.

RICHARD

Hard to know me? I sent you from Rome the chapters of my book as I wrote them; and letters for nine long years. Well, eight years.

BEATRICE

Yes, it was nearly a year before your first letter came.

RICHARD

It was answered at once by you. And from that on you have watched me in my struggle. [*Joins his hands earnestly.*] Tell me, Miss Justice, did you feel that what you read was written for your eyes? Or that you inspired me?

BEATRICE

[*Shakes her head.*] I need not answer that question.

RICHARD

What then?

18

BEATRICE

[Is silent for a moment.] I cannot say it. You yourself must ask me, Mr Rowan.

RICHARD

[With some vehemence.] Then that I expressed in those chapters and letters, and in my character and life as well, something in your soul which you could not – pride or scorn?

BEATRICE

Could not?

RICHARD

[Leans towards her.] Could not because you dared not. Is that why?

BEATRICE

[Bends her head.] Yes.

RICHARD

On account of others or for want of courage – which?

BEATRICE

[Softly.] Courage.

RICHARD

[Slowly.] And so you have followed me with pride and scorn also in your heart?

BEATRICE

And loneliness.

> [She leans her head on her hand, averting her face. RICH-ARD rises and walks slowly to the window on the left. He looks out for some moments and then returns towards her, crosses to the lounge and sits down near her.]

RICHARD

Do you love him still?

BEATRICE

I do not even know.

RICHARD

It was that that made me so reserved with you – then – even though I felt your interest in me, even though I felt that I too was something in your life.

BEATRICE

You were.

RICHARD

Yet that separated me from you. I was a third person, I felt. Your names were always spoken together, Robert and Beatrice, as long as I can remember. It seemed to me, to everyone . . .

BEATRICE

We are first cousins. It is not strange that we were often together.

RICHARD

He told me of your secret engagement with him. He had no secrets from me; I suppose you know that.

BEATRICE

[*Uneasily.*] What happened – between us – is so long ago. I was a child.

RICHARD

[*Smiles maliciously.*] A child? Are you sure? It was in the garden of his mother's house. No? [*He points towards the garden.*] Over there. You plighted your troth, as they say, with a kiss. And you gave him your garter. Is it allowed to mention that?

BEATRICE

[*With some reserve.*] If you think it worthy of mention.

RICHARD

I think I have not forgotten it. [*Clasping his hands quietly.*] I do not understand it. I thought, too, that after I had gone . . . Did my going make you suffer?

BEATRICE

I always knew you would go some day. I did not suffer; only I was changed.

RICHARD

Towards him?

BEATRICE

Everything was changed. His life, his mind, even, seemed to change after that.

RICHARD

[*Musing.*] Yes. I saw that you had changed when I received your first letter after a year; after your illness, too. You even said so in your letter.

BEATRICE

It brought me near to death. It made me see things differently.

RICHARD

And so a coldness began between you, little by little. Is that it?

BEATRICE

[*Half closing her eyes.*] No. Not at once. I saw in him a pale reflection of you: then that too faded. Of what good is it to talk now?

RICHARD

[*With a repressed energy.*] But what is this that seems to hang over you? It cannot be so tragic.

BEATRICE

[*Calmly.*] O, not in the least tragic. I shall become gradually better, they tell me, as I grow older. As I did not die then they tell me I shall probably live. I am given life and health again – when I cannot use them. [*Calmly and bitterly.*] I am convalescent.

RICHARD

[*Gently.*] Does nothing then in life give you peace? Surely it exists for you somewhere.

BEATRICE

If there were convents in our religion perhaps there. At least, I think so at times.

RICHARD

[*Shakes his head.*] No, Miss Justice, not even there. You could not give yourself freely and wholly.

BEATRICE

[*Looking at him.*] I would try.

RICHARD

You would try, yes. You were drawn to him as your mind was drawn towards mine. You held back from him. From me, too, in a different way. You cannot give yourself freely and wholly.

BEATRICE

[*Joins her hands softly.*] It is a terribly hard thing to do, Mr Rowan – to give oneself freely and wholly – and be happy.

RICHARD

But do you feel that happiness is the best, the highest that we can know.

BEATRICE

[*With fervour.*] I wish I could feel it.

RICHARD

[*Leans back, his hands locked together behind his head.*] O, if you knew how I am suffering at this moment! For your case, too. But suffering most of all for my own. [*With bitter force.*] And how I pray that I may be granted again my dead mother's hardness of heart! For some help, within me or without, I must find. And find it I will.

[BEATRICE *rises, looks at him intently, and walks away towards the garden door. She turns with indecision, looks again at him and, coming back, leans over the easychair.*]

BEATRICE

[*Quietly.*] Did she send for you before she died, Mr Rowan?

RICHARD

[*Lost in thought.*] Who?

BEATRICE

Your mother.

RICHARD

[*Recovering himself, looks keenly at her for a moment.*] So that, too, was said of me here by my friends – that she sent for me before she died and that I did not go?

BEATRICE

Yes.

RICHARD

[*Coldly.*] She did not. She died alone, not having forgiven me, and fortified by the rites of holy church.

BEATRICE

Mr Rowan, why do you speak to me in such a way?

RICHARD

[*Rises and walks nervously to and fro.*] And what I suffer at this moment you will say is my punishment.

BEATRICE

Did she write to you? I mean before . . .

RICHARD

[*Halting.*] Yes. A letter of warning, bidding me break with the past, and remember her last words to me.

BEATRICE

[*Softly.*] And does death not move you, Mr Rowan? It is an end. Everything else is so uncertain.

RICHARD

While she lived she turned aside from me and from mine. That is certain.

BEATRICE

From you and from . . .

RICHARD

From Bertha and from me and from our child. And so I waited for the end as you say; and it came.

23

BEATRICE

[*Covers her face with her hands.*] O no. Surely no.

RICHARD

[*Fiercely.*] How can my words hurt her poor body that rots in the grave? Do you think I do not pity her cold blighted love for me? I fought against her spirit while she lived to the bitter end. [*He presses his hand to his forehead.*] It fights against me still – in here.

BEATRICE

[*As before.*] O, do not speak like that.

RICHARD

She drove me away. On account of her I lived years in exile and poverty too, or near it. I never accepted the doles she sent me through the bank. I waited, too, not for her death but for some understanding of me, her own son, her own flesh and blood; that never came.

BEATRICE

Not even after Archie . . .?

RICHARD

[*Rudely.*] My son, you think? A child of sin and shame! Are you serious? [*She raises her face and looks at him.*] There were tongues here ready to tell her all, to embitter her withering mind still more against me and Bertha and our godless nameless child. [*Holding out his hands to her.*] Can you not hear her mocking me while I speak? You must know the voice, surely, the voice that called you *the black protestant,* the pervert's daughter. [*With sudden selfcontrol.*] In any case a remarkable woman.

BEATRICE

[*Weakly.*] At least you are free now.

RICHARD

[*Nods.*] Yes, she could not alter the terms of my father's will nor live for ever.

BEATRICE

[*With joined hands.*] They are both gone now, Mr Rowan. They both loved you, believe me. Their last thoughts were of you.

RICHARD

[*Approaching, touches her lightly on the shoulder, and points to the crayon drawing on the wall.*] Do you see him there, smiling and handsome? His last thoughts! I remember the night he died. [*He pauses for an instant and then goes on calmly.*] I was a boy of fourteen. He called me to his bedside. He knew I wanted to go to the theatre to hear *Carmen*. He told my mother to give me a shilling. I kissed him and went. When I came home he was dead. Those were his last thoughts as far as I know.

BEATRICE

The hardness of heart you prayed for . . . [*She breaks off.*]

RICHARD

[*Unheeding.*] That is my last memory of him. Is there not something sweet and noble in it?

BEATRICE

Mr Rowan, something is on your mind to make you speak like this. Something has changed you since you came back three months ago.

RICHARD

[*Gazing again at the drawing, calmly, almost gaily.*] He will help me, perhaps, my smiling handsome father.

[*A knock is heard at the hall door on the left.*]

RICHARD

[*Suddenly.*] No, no. Not the smiler, Miss Justice. The old mother. It is her spirit I need. I am going.

BEATRICE

Someone knocked. They have come back.

RICHARD

No, Bertha has a key. It is he. At least, I am going, whoever it is.

[*He goes out quickly on the left and comes back at once with his straw hat in his hand.*]

BEATRICE

He? Who?

25

RICHARD

O, probably Robert. I am going out through the garden. I cannot see him now. Say I have gone to the post. Goodbye.

BEATRICE

[*With growing alarm.*] It is Robert you do not wish to see?

RICHARD

[*Quietly.*] For the moment, yes. This talk has upset me. Ask him to wait.

BEATRICE

You will come back?

RICHARD

Please God.

[*He goes out quickly through the garden.* BEATRICE *makes as if to follow him and then stops after a few paces.* BRIGID *enters by the folding doors on the right and goes out on the left. The hall door is heard opening. A few seconds after* BRIGID *enters with* ROBERT HAND. ROBERT HAND *is a middlesized, rather stout man between thirty and forty. He is cleanshaven, with mobile features. His hair and eyes are dark and his complexion sallow. His gait and speech are rather slow. He wears a dark blue morning suit and carries in his hand a large bunch of red roses wrapped in tissue paper.*]

ROBERT

[*Coming towards her with outstretched hand which she takes.*] My dearest coz! Brigid told me you were here. I had no notion. Did you send mother a telegram?

BEATRICE

[*Gazing at the roses.*] No.

ROBERT

[*Following her gaze.*] You are admiring my roses. I brought them to the mistress of the house. [*Critically.*] I am afraid they are not mine.

BRIGID

O, they are lovely, sir. The mistress will be delighted with them.

ROBERT

[*Lays the roses carelessly on a chair out of sight.*] Is nobody in?

BRIGID

Yes, sir. Sit down, sir. They'll be here now any moment. The master was here.

> [*She looks about her and with a half curtsey goes out on the right.*]

ROBERT

[*After a short silence.*] How are you, Beatty? And how are all down in Youghal? As dull as ever?

BEATRICE

They were well when I left.

ROBERT

[*Politely.*] O, but I'm sorry I did not know you were coming. I would have met you at the train. Why did you do it? You have some queer ways about you, Beatty, haven't you?

BEATRICE

[*In the same tone.*] Thank you, Robert. I am quite used to getting about alone.

ROBERT

Yes, but I mean to say ... O, well you have arrived in your own characteristic way.

> [*A noise is heard at the window and a boy's voice is heard calling, 'Mr Hand!'* ROBERT *turns.*]

By Jove, Archie, too, is arriving in a characteristic way!

> [ARCHIE *scrambles into the room through the open window on the left and then rises to his feet, flushed and panting.* ARCHIE *is a boy of eight years, dressed in white breeches, jersey and cap. He wears spectacles, has a lively manner and speaks with the slight trace of a foreign accent.*]

BEATRICE

[*Going towards him.*] Goodness gracious, Archie! What is the matter?

ARCHIE

[*Rising, out of breath.*] Eh! I ran all the avenue.

ROBERT

[*Smiles and holds out his hand.*] Good evening, Archie. Why did you run?

ARCHIE

[*Shakes hands.*] Good evening. We saw you on the top of the tram, and I shouted *Mr Hand!* But you did not see me. But we saw you, mamma and I. She will be here in a minute. I ran.

BEATRICE

[*Holding out her hand.*] And poor me!

ARCHIE

[*Shakes hands somewhat shyly.*] Good evening, Miss Justice.

BEATRICE

Were you disappointed that I did not come last Friday for the lesson?

ARCHIE

[*Glancing at her, smiles.*] No.

BEATRICE

Glad?

ARCHIE

[*Suddenly.*] But today it is too late.

BEATRICE

A very short lesson?

ARCHIE

[*Pleased.*] Yes.

BEATRICE

But now you must study, Archie.

ROBERT

Were you at the bath?

ARCHIE

Yes.

ROBERT

Are you a good swimmer now?

ARCHIE

[*Leans against the davenport.*] No, mamma won't let me into the deep place. Can you swim well, Mr Hand?

ROBERT

Splendidly. Like a stone.

ARCHIE

[*Laughs.*] Like a stone! [*Pointing down.*] Down that way?

ROBERT

[*Pointing.*] Yes, down; straight down. How do you say that over in Italy?

ARCHIE

That? *Giù.* [*Pointing down and up.*] That is *giù* and this is *sù.* Do you want to speak to my pappie?

ROBERT

Yes. I came to see him.

ARCHIE

[*Going towards the study.*] I will tell him. He is in there, writing.

BEATRICE

[*Calmly, looking at* ROBERT.] No; he is out. He is gone to the post with some letters.

ROBERT

[*Lightly.*] O, never mind. I will wait if he is only gone to the post.

ARCHIE

But mamma is coming. [*He glances towards the window.*] Here she is!

[ARCHIE *runs out by the door on the left.* BEATRICE *walks slowly towards the davenport.* ROBERT *remains standing. A short silence.* ARCHIE *and* BERTHA *come in through the door on the left.* BERTHA *is a young woman of graceful build. She has dark grey eyes, patient in*

29

*expression, and soft features. Her manner is cordial and
self-possessed. She wears a lavender dress and carries her
cream gloves knotted round the handle of her sunshade.*]

BERTHA

[*Shaking hands.*] Good evening, Miss Justice. We thought
you were still down in Youghal.

BEATRICE

[*Shaking hands.*] Good evening, Mrs Rowan.

BERTHA

[*Bows.*] Good evening, Mr Hand.

ROBERT

[*Bowing.*] Good evening, *signora!* Just imagine, I didn't know
either she was back till I found her here.

BERTHA

[*To both.*] Did you not come together?

BEATRICE

No. I came first. Mr Rowan was going out. He said you would
be back any moment.

BERTHA

I'm sorry. If you had written or sent over word by the girl
this morning ...

BEATRICE

[*Laughs nervously.*] I arrived only an hour and a half ago. I
thought of sending a telegram but it seemed too tragic.

BERTHA

Ah? Only now you arrived?

ROBERT

[*Extending his arms, blandly.*] I retire from public and
private life. Her first cousin and a journalist, I know nothing
of her movements.

BEATRICE

[*Not directly to him.*] My movements are not very interesting.

ROBERT

[*In the same tone.*] A lady's movements are always interesting.

BERTHA

But sit down, won't you? You must be very tired.

BEATRICE

[*Quickly.*] No, not at all. I just came for Archie's lesson.

BERTHA

I wouldn't hear of such a thing, Miss Justice, after your long journey.

ARCHIE

[*Suddenly to* BEATRICE.] And, besides, you didn't bring the music.

BEATRICE

[*A little confused.*] That I forgot. But we have the old piece.

ROBERT

[*Pinching* ARCHIE's *ear.*] You little scamp. You want to get off the lesson.

BERTHA

O, never mind the lesson. You must sit down and have a cup of tea now. [*Going towards the door on the right.*] I'll tell Brigid.

ARCHIE

I will, mamma. [*He makes a movement to go.*]

BEATRICE

No, please Mrs Rowan. Archie! I would really prefer . . .

ROBERT

[*Quietly.*] I suggest a compromise. Let it be a half-lesson.

BERTHA

But she must be exhausted.

BEATRICE

[*Quickly.*] Not in the least. I was thinking of the lesson in the train.

ROBERT

[To BERTHA.] You see what it is to have a conscience, Mrs Rowan?

ARCHIE

Of my lesson, Miss Justice?

BEATRICE

[Simply.] It is ten days since I heard the sound of a piano.

BERTHA

O, very well. If that is it . . .

ROBERT

[Nervously, gaily.] Let us have the piano by all means. I know what is in Beatty's ears at this moment. [To BEATRICE.] Shall I tell?

BEATRICE

If you know.

ROBERT

The buzz of the harmonium in her father's parlour. [To BEATRICE.] Confess.

BEATRICE

[Smiling.] Yes. I can hear it.

ROBERT

[Grimly.] So can I. The asthmatic voice of protestantism.

BERTHA

Did you not enjoy yourself down there, Miss Justice?

ROBERT

[Intervenes.] She did not, Mrs Rowan. She goes there on retreat, when the protestant strain in her prevails – gloom, seriousness, righteousness.

BEATRICE

I go to see my father.

ROBERT

[Continuing.] But she comes back here to my mother, you see. The piano influence is from our side of the house.

BERTHA

[*Hesitating.*] Well, Miss Justice, if you would like to play something . . . But please don't fatigue yourself with Archie.

ROBERT

[*Suavely.*] Do, Beatty. That is what you want.

BEATRICE

If Archie will come?

ARCHIE

[*With a shrug.*] To listen.

BEATRICE

[*Takes his hand.*] And a little lesson, too. Very short.

BERTHA

Well, afterwards you must stay to tea.

BEATRICE

[*To* ARCHIE.] Come.

[BEATRICE *and* ARCHIE *go out together by the door on the left.* BERTHA *goes towards the davenport, takes off her hat and lays it with her sunshade on the desk. Then taking a key from a little flowervase, she opens a drawer of the davenport, takes out a slip of paper and closes the drawer again.* ROBERT *stands watching her.*]

BERTHA

[*Coming towards him with the paper in her hand.*] You put this into my hand last night. What does it mean?

ROBERT

Do you not know?

BERTHA

[*Reads.*] There is one word which I have never dared to say to you. What is the word?

ROBERT

That I have a deep liking for you.

[*A short pause. The piano is heard faintly from the upper room.*]

33

ROBERT

[*Takes the bunch of roses from the chair.*] I brought these for you. Will you take them from me?

BERTHA

[*Taking them.*] Thank you. [*She lays them on the table and unfolds the paper again.*] Why did you not dare to say it last night?

ROBERT

I could not speak to you or follow you. There were too many people on the lawn. I wanted you to think over it and so I put it into your hand when you were going away.

BERTHA

Now you have dared to say it.

ROBERT

[*Moves his hands slowly past his eyes.*] You passed. The avenue was dim with dusky light. I could see the dark green masses of the trees. And you passed beyond them. You were like the moon.

BERTHA

[*Laughs.*] Why like the moon?

ROBERT

In that dress, with your slim body, walking with little even steps. I saw the moon passing in the dusk till you passed and left my sight.

BERTHA

Did you think of me last night?

ROBERT

[*Comes nearer.*] I think of you always – as something beautiful and distant – the moon or some deep music.

BERTHA

[*Smiling.*] And last night which was I?

ROBERT

I was awake half the night. I could hear your voice. I could see your face in the dark. Your eyes ... I want to speak to you. Will you listen to me? May I speak?

BERTHA

[*Sitting down.*] You may.

ROBERT

[*Sitting beside her.*] Are you annoyed with me?

BERTHA

No.

ROBERT

I thought you were. You put away my poor flowers so quickly.

BERTHA

[*Takes them from the table and holds them close to her face.*] Is this what you wish me to do with them?

ROBERT

[*Watching her.*] Your face is a flower too – but more beautiful. A wild flower blowing in a hedge. [*Moving his chair closer to her.*] Why are you smiling? At my words?

BERTHA

[*Laying the flowers in her lap.*] I am wondering if that is what you say – to the others.

ROBERT

[*Surprised.*] What others?

BERTHA

The other women. I hear you have so many admirers.

ROBERT

[*Involuntarily.*] And that is why you too . . .?

BERTHA

But you have, haven't you?

ROBERT

Friends, yes.

BERTHA

Do you speak to them in the same way?

ROBERT

[*In an offended tone.*] How can you ask me such a question?

35

What kind of a person do you think I am? Or why do you listen to me? Did you not like me to speak to you in that way?

BERTHA

What you said was very kind. [*She looks at him for a moment.*] Thank you for saying it – and thinking it.

ROBERT

[*Leaning forward.*] Bertha!

BERTHA

Yes?

ROBERT

I have the right to call you by your name. From old times – nine years ago. We were Bertha – and Robert – then. Can we not be so now, too?

BERTHA

[*Readily.*] O yes. Why should we not?

ROBERT

Bertha, you knew. From the very night you landed on Kingstown pier. It all came back to me then. And you knew it. You saw it.

BERTHA

No. Not that night.

ROBERT

When?

BERTHA

The night we landed I felt very tired and dirty. [*Shaking her head.*] I did not see it in you that night.

ROBERT

[*Smiling.*] Tell me what did you see that night – your very first impression.

BERTHA

[*Knitting her brows.*] You were standing with your back to the gangway, talking to two ladies.

ROBERT

To two plain middleaged ladies, yes.

36

BERTHA

I recognized you at once. And I saw that you had got fat.

ROBERT

[*Takes her hand.*] And this poor fat Robert – do you dislike him then so much? Do you disbelieve all he says?

BERTHA

I think men speak like that to all women whom they like or admire. What do you want me to believe?

ROBERT

All men, Bertha?

BERTHA

[*With sudden sadness.*] I think so.

ROBERT

I too?

BERTHA

Yes, Robert. I think you too.

ROBERT

All then – without exception? Or with one exception? [*In a lower tone.*] Or is he too – Richard too – like us all – in that at least? Or different?

BERTHA

[*Looks into his eyes.*] Different.

ROBERT

Are you quite sure, Bertha?

BERTHA

[*A little confused, tries to withdraw her hand.*] I have answered you.

ROBERT

[*Suddenly.*] Bertha, may I kiss your hand? Let me. May I?

BERTHA

If you wish.

[*He lifts her hand to his lips slowly. She rises suddenly and listens.*]

37

BERTHA
Did you hear the garden gate?

ROBERT
[Rising also.] No.

[A short pause. The piano can be heard faintly from the
upper room.]

ROBERT
[Pleading.] Do not go away. You must never go away now.
Your life is here. I came for that too today – to speak to him –
to urge him to accept this position. He must. And you must
persuade him. You have a great influence over him.

BERTHA
You want him to remain here.

ROBERT
Yes.

BERTHA
Why?

ROBERT
For your sake because you are unhappy so far away. For his
too because he should think of his future.

BERTHA
[Laughing.] Do you remember what he said when you spoke
to him last night?

ROBERT
About . . .? [Reflecting.] Yes. He quoted the Our Father about
our daily bread. He said that to take care for the future is to
destroy hope and love in the world.

BERTHA
Do you not think he is strange?

ROBERT
In that, yes.

BERTHA
A little – mad?

ROBERT

[*Comes closer.*] No. He is not. Perhaps we are. Why, do you . . .?

BERTHA

[*Laughs.*] I ask you because you are intelligent.

ROBERT

You must not go away. I will not let you.

BERTHA

[*Looks full at him.*] You?

ROBERT

Those eyes must not go away. [*He takes her hands.*] May I kiss your eyes?

BERTHA

Do so.

> [*He kisses her eyes and then passes his hand over her hair.*]

ROBERT

Little Bertha!

BERTHA

[*Smiling.*] But I am not so little. Why do you call me little?

ROBERT

Little Bertha! One embrace? [*He puts his arm around her.*] Look into my eyes again.

BERTHA

[*Looks.*] I can see the little gold spots. So many you have.

ROBERT

[*Delighted.*] Your voice! Give me a kiss, a kiss with your mouth.

BERTHA

Take it.

ROBERT

I am afraid. [*He kisses her mouth and passes his hand many times over her hair.*] At last I hold you in my arms!

BERTHA

And are you satisfied?

ROBERT

Let me feel your lips touch mine.

BERTHA

And then you will be satisfied?

ROBERT

[*Murmurs.*] Your lips, Bertha!

BERTHA

[*Closes her eyes and kisses him quickly.*] There. [*Puts her hands on his shoulders.*] Why don't you say: thanks.

ROBERT

[*Sighs.*] My life is finished – over.

BERTHA

O don't speak like that now, Robert.

ROBERT

Over, over. I want to end it and have done with it.

BERTHA

[*Concerned but light.*] You silly fellow!

ROBERT

[*Presses her to him.*] To end it all – death. To fall from a great high cliff, down, right down into the sea.

BERTHA

Please, Robert . . .

ROBERT

Listening to music and in the arms of the woman I love – the sea, music and death.

BERTHA

[*Looks at him for a moment.*] The woman you love?

ROBERT

[*Hurriedly.*] I want to speak to you, Bertha – alone – not here. Will you come?

BERTHA

[*With downcast eyes.*] I too want to speak to you.

ROBERT

[*Tenderly.*] Yes, dear, I know. [*He kisses her again.*] I will speak to you; tell you all, then. I will kiss you, then, long long kisses – when you come to me – long long sweet kisses.

BERTHA

Where?

ROBERT

[*In the tone of passion.*] Your eyes. Your lips. All your divine body.

BERTHA

[*Repelling his embrace, confused.*] I meant where do you wish me to come.

ROBERT

To my house. Not my mother's over there. I will write the address for you. Will you come?

BERTHA

When?

ROBERT

Tonight. Between eight and nine. Come. I will wait for you tonight. And every night. You will?

[*He kisses her with passion, holding her head between his hands. After a few instants she breaks from him. He sits down.*]

BERTHA

[*Listening.*] The gate opened.

ROBERT

[*Intensely.*] I will wait for you.

[*He takes the slip from the table.* BERTHA *moves away from him slowly.* RICHARD *comes in from the garden.*]

RICHARD

[*Advancing, takes off his hat.*] Good afternoon.

ROBERT

[*Rises, with nervous friendliness.*] Good afternoon, Richard.

BERTHA

[*At the table, taking the roses.*] Look what lovely roses Mr Hand brought me.

ROBERT

I am afraid they are overblown.

RICHARD

[*Suddenly.*] Excuse me for a moment, will you?

> [*He turns and goes into his study quickly.* ROBERT *takes a pencil from his pocket and writes a few words on the slip; then hands it quickly to* BERTHA.]

ROBERT

[*Rapidly.*] The address. Take the tram at Lansdowne Road and ask to be let down near there.

BERTHA

[*Takes it.*] I promise nothing.

ROBERT

I will wait.

> [RICHARD *comes back from the study.*]

BERTHA

[*Going.*] I must put these roses in water.

RICHARD

[*Handing her his hat.*] Yes, do. And please put my hat on the rack.

BERTHA

[*Takes it.*] So I will leave you to yourselves for your talk. [*Looking round.*] Do you want anything? Cigarettes?

RICHARD

Thanks. We have them here.

BERTHA

Then I can go?

> [*She goes out on the left with* RICHARD's *hat, which she leaves in the hall, and returns at once; she stops for a*

moment at the davenport, replaces the slip in the
drawer, locks it, and replaces the key, and, taking the
roses, goes towards the right. ROBERT precedes her to
open the door for her. She bows and goes out.]

RICHARD

[Points to the chair near the little table on the right.] Your
place of honour.

ROBERT

[Sits down.] Thanks. [Passing his hand over his brow.] Good
Lord, how warm it is today! The heat pains me here in the
eye. The glare.

RICHARD

The room is rather dark, I think, with the blind down but if
you wish ...

ROBERT

[Quickly.] Not at all. I know what it is – the result of night
work.

RICHARD

[Sits on the lounge.] Must you?

ROBERT

[Sighs.] Eh, yes. I must see part of the paper through every
night. And then my leading articles. We are approaching a
difficult moment. And not only here.

RICHARD

[After a slight pause.] Have you any news?

ROBERT

[In a different voice.] Yes. I want to speak to you seriously.
Today may be an important day for you – or rather, tonight.
I saw the vicechancellor this morning. He has the highest
opinion of you, Richard. He has read your book, he said.

RICHARD

Did he buy it or borrow it?

ROBERT

Bought it, I hope.

43

I shall smoke a cigarette. Thirtyseven copies have now been sold in Dublin.

[*He takes a cigarette from the box on the table, and lights it.*]

ROBERT

[*Suavely, hopelessly.*] Well, the matter is closed for the present. You have your iron mask on today.

RICHARD

[*Smoking.*] Let me hear the rest.

ROBERT

[*Again seriously.*] Richard, you are too suspicious. It is a defect in you. He assured me he has the highest possible opinion of you, as everyone has. You are the man for the post, he says. In fact, he told me that, if your name goes forward, he will work might and main for you with the senate and I . . . will do my part, of course, in the press and privately. I regard it as a public duty. The chair of romance literature is yours by right, as a scholar, as a literary personality.

RICHARD

The conditions?

ROBERT

Conditions? You mean about the future?

RICHARD

I mean about the past.

ROBERT

[*Easily.*] That episode in your past is forgotten. An act of impulse. We are all impulsive.

RICHARD

[*Looks fixedly at him.*] You called it an act of folly, then – nine years ago. You told me I was hanging a weight about my neck.

44

ROBERT

I was wrong. [*Suavely.*] Here is how the matter stands, Richard. Everyone knows that you ran away years ago with a young girl ... How shall I put it? ... with a young girl not exactly your equal. [*Kindly.*] Excuse me, Richard, that is not my opinion nor my language. I am simply using the language of people whose opinions I don't share.

RICHARD

Writing one of your leading articles, in fact.

ROBERT

Put it so. Well, it made a great sensation at the time. A mysterious disappearance. My name was involved too, as best man, let us say, on that famous occasion. Of course, they think I acted from a mistaken sense of friendship. Well, all that is known. [*With some hesitation.*] But what happened afterwards is not known.

RICHARD

No?

ROBERT

Of course, it is your affair, Richard. However, you are not so young now as you were then. The expression is quite in the style of my leading articles, isn't it?

RICHARD

Do you, or do you not, want me to give the lie to my past life?

ROBERT

I am thinking of your future life – here. I understand your pride and your sense of liberty. I understand their point of view also. However, there is a way out; it is simply this. Refrain from contradicting any rumours you may hear concerning what happened ... or did not happen after you went away. Leave the rest to me.

RICHARD

You will set these rumours afloat?

ROBERT

I will. God help me.

45

RICHARD

[*Observing him.*] For the sake of social conventions?

ROBERT

For the sake of something else too – our friendship, our life-long friendship.

RICHARD

Thanks.

ROBERT

[*Slightly wounded.*] And I will tell you the whole truth.

RICHARD

[*Smiles and bows.*] Yes. Do, please.

ROBERT

Not only for your sake. Also for the sake of – your present partner in life.

RICHARD

I see.

[*He crushes his cigarette softly on the ashtray and then leans forward, rubbing his hands slowly.*]

RICHARD

Why for her sake?

ROBERT

[*Also leans forward, quietly.*] Richard, have you been quite fair to her? It was her own free choice, you will say. But was she really free to choose? She was a mere girl. She accepted all that you proposed.

RICHARD

[*Smiles.*] That is your way of saying that she proposed what I would not accept.

ROBERT

[*Nods.*] I remember. And she went away with you. But was it of her own free choice? Answer me frankly.

RICHARD

[*Turns to him, calmly.*] I played for her against all that you say or can say; and I won.

ROBERT
[Nodding again.] Yes, you won.

RICHARD
[Rises.] Excuse me for forgetting. Will you have some whisky?

ROBERT
All things come to those who wait.

> [RICHARD goes to the sideboard and brings a small tray with the decanter and glasses to the table where he sets it down.]

RICHARD
[Sits down again, leaning back on the lounge.] Will you please help yourself?

ROBERT
[Does so.] And you? Steadfast? [RICHARD shakes his head.] Lord, when I think of our wild nights long ago – talks by the hour, plans, carouses, revelry . . .

RICHARD
In our house.

ROBERT
It is mine now. I have kept it ever since though I don't go there often. Whenever you like to come let me know. You must come some night. It will be old times again. [He lifts his glass and drinks.] Prosit!

RICHARD
It was not only a house of revelry; it was to be the hearth of a new life. [Musing.] And in that name all our sins were committed.

ROBERT
Sins! Drinking and blasphemy [he points] by me. And drinking and heresy, much worse, [he points again] by you – are those the sins you mean?

RICHARD
And some others.

ROBERT

[*Lightly, uneasily.*] You mean the women. I have no remorse of conscience. Maybe you have. We had two keys on those occasions. [*Maliciously.*] Have you?

RICHARD

[*Irritated.*] For you it was all quite natural?

ROBERT

For me it is quite natural to kiss a woman whom I like. Why not? She is beautiful for me.

RICHARD

[*Toying with the lounge cushion.*] Do you kiss everything that is beautiful for you?

ROBERT

Everything – if it can be kissed. [*He takes up a flat stone which lies on the table.*] This stone, for instance. It is so cool, so polished, so delicate, like a woman's temple. It is silent, it suffers our passion; and it is beautiful. [*He places it against his lips.*] And so I kiss it because it is beautiful. And what is a woman? A work of nature, too, like a stone or a flower or a bird. A kiss is an act of homage.

RICHARD

It is an act of union between man and woman. Even if we are often led to desire through the sense of beauty can you say that the beautiful is what we desire?

ROBERT

[*Pressing the stone to his forehead.*] You will give me a headache if you make me think today. I cannot think today. I feel too natural, too common. After all, what is most attractive in even the most beautiful woman?

RICHARD

What?

ROBERT

Not those qualities which she has and other women have not but the qualities which she has in common with them. I mean ... the commonest. [*Turning over the stone, he presses*

the other side to his forehead.] I mean how her body develops
heat when it is pressed, the movement of her blood, how
quickly she changes by digestion what she eats into – what
shall be nameless. [*Laughing.*] I am very common today.
Perhaps that idea never struck you?

RICHARD

[*Drily.*] Many ideas strike a man who has lived nine years
with a woman.

ROBERT

Yes. I suppose they do . . . This beautiful cool stone does me
good. Is it a paperweight or a cure for headache?

RICHARD

Bertha brought it home one day from the strand. She, too,
says that it is beautiful.

ROBERT

[*Lays down the stone quietly.*] She is right.

[*He raises his glass and drinks. A pause.*]

RICHARD

Is that all you wanted to say to me?

ROBERT

[*Quickly.*] There is something else. The vicechancellor sends
you, through me, an invitation for tonight – to dinner at his
house. You know where he lives? [RICHARD *nods.*] I thought
you might have forgotten. Strictly private, of course. He
wants to meet you again and sends you a very warm invitation.

RICHARD

For what hour?

ROBERT

Eight. But, like yourself, he is free and easy about time. Now,
Richard, you must go there. That is all. I feel tonight will be
the turning point in your life. You will live here and work
here and think here and be honoured here – among our
people.

RICHARD

[*Smiling.*] I can almost see two envoys starting for the United
States to collect funds for my statue a hundred years hence.

49

ROBERT

[*Agreeably.*] Once I made a little epigram about statues. All statues are of two kinds. [*He folds his arms across his chest.*] The statue which says: *How shall I get down?* and the other kind [*he unfolds his arms and extends his right arm, averting his head*] the statue which says: *In my time the dunghill was so high.*

RICHARD

The second one for me, please.

ROBERT

[*Lazily.*] Will you give me one of those long cigars of yours?

[RICHARD *selects a Virginia cigar from the box on the table and hands it to him with the straw drawn out.*]

ROBERT

[*Lighting it.*] These cigars Europeanize me. If Ireland is to become a new Ireland she must first become European. And that is what you are here for, Richard. Some day we shall have to choose between England and Europe. I am a descendant of the dark foreigners: that is why I like to be here. I may be childish. But where else in Dublin can I get a bandit cigar like this or a cup of black coffee? The man who drinks black coffee is going to conquer Ireland. And now I will take just a half measure of that whisky, Richard, to show you there is no ill feeling.

RICHARD

[*Points.*] Help yourself.

ROBERT

[*Does so.*] Thanks. [*He drinks and goes on as before.*] Then you yourself, the way you loll on that lounge: then your boy's voice and also – Bertha herself. Do you allow me to call her that, Richard? I mean as an old friend of both of you.

RICHARD

O why not?

ROBERT

[*With animation.*] You have that fierce indignation which lacerated the heart of Swift. You have fallen from a higher

50

world, Richard, and you are filled with fierce indignation when you find that life is cowardly and ignoble. While I . . . shall I tell you?

RICHARD

By all means.

ROBERT

[*Archly.*] I have come up from a lower world and I am filled with astonishment when I find that people have any redeeming virtue at all.

RICHARD

[*Sits up suddenly and leans his elbows on the table.*] You are my friend, then?

ROBERT

[*Gravely.*] I fought for you all the time you were away. I fought to bring you back. I fought to keep your place for you here. I will fight for you still because I have faith in you, the faith of a disciple in his master. I cannot say more than that. It may seem strange to you . . . Give me a match.

RICHARD

[*Lights and offers him a match.*] There is a faith still stranger than the faith of the disciple in his master.

ROBERT

And that is?

RICHARD

The faith of a master in the disciple who will betray him.

ROBERT

The church lost a theologian in you, Richard. But I think you look too deeply into life. [*He rises, pressing* RICHARD's *arms slightly.*] Be gay. Life is not worth it.

RICHARD

[*Without rising.*] Are you going?

ROBERT

Must. [*He turns and says in a friendly tone.*] Then it is all arranged. We meet tonight at the vicechancellor's. I shall look in at about ten. So you can have an hour or so to yourselves first. You will wait till I come?

RICHARD

Good.

ROBERT

One more match and I am happy.

[RICHARD *strikes another match, hands it to him and rises also.* ARCHIE *comes in by the door on the left followed by* BEATRICE.]

ROBERT

Congratulate me, Beatty. I have won over Richard.

ARCHIE

[*Crossing to the door on the right, calls.*] Mamma, Miss Justice is going.

BEATRICE

On what are you to be congratulated?

ROBERT

On a victory, of course. [*Laying his hand lightly on* RICHARD's *shoulder.*] The descendant of Archibald Hamilton Rowan has come home.

RICHARD

I am not a descendant of Hamilton Rowan.

ROBERT

What matter?

[BERTHA *comes in from the right with a bowl of roses.*]

BEATRICE

Has Mr Rowan ... ?'

ROBERT

[*Turning towards* BERTHA.] Richard is coming tonight to the vicechancellor's dinner. The fatted calf will be eaten: roast, I hope. And next session will see the descendant of a namesake of etcetera, etcetera in a chair of the university. [*He offers his hand.*] Good afternoon, Richard. We shall meet tonight.

RICHARD

[*Touches his hand.*] At Philippi.

BEATRICE

[*Shakes hands also.*] Accept my best wishes, Mr Rowan.

RICHARD

Thanks. But do not believe him.

ROBERT

[*Vivaciously.*] Believe me, believe me. [*To* BERTHA.] Good afternoon, Mrs Rowan.

BERTHA

[*Shaking hands, candidly.*] I thank you, too. [*To* BEATRICE.] You won't stay to tea, Miss Justice?

BEATRICE

No, thank you. [*Takes leave of her.*] I must go. Good afternoon. Goodbye, Archie [*going*].

ROBERT

Addio, Archibald.

ARCHIE

Addio.

ROBERT

Wait, Beatty. I shall accompany you.

BEATRICE

[*Going out on the right with* BERTHA.] Oh, don't trouble.

ROBERT

[*Following her.*] But I insist – as a cousin.

[BERTHA, BEATRICE, *and* ROBERT *go out by the door on the left.* RICHARD *stands irresolutely near the table.* ARCHIE *closes the door leading to the hall and, coming over to him, plucks him by the sleeve.*]

ARCHIE

I say, pappie!

RICHARD

[*Absently.*] What is it?

53

I want to ask you a thing.

RICHARD

[*Sitting on the end of the lounge, stares in front of him.*] What is it?

ARCHIE

Will you ask mamma to let me go out in the morning with the milkman?

RICHARD

With the milkman?

ARCHIE

Yes. In the milkcar. He says he will let me drive when we get on to the roads where there are no people. The horse is a very good beast. Can I go?

RICHARD

Yes.

ARCHIE

Ask mamma now can I go. Will you?

RICHARD

[*Glances towards the door.*] I will.

ARCHIE

He said he will show me the cows he has in the field. Do you know how many cows he has?

RICHARD

How many?

ARCHIE

Eleven. Eight red and three white. But one is sick now. No, not sick. But it fell.

RICHARD

Cows?

ARCHIE

[*With a gesture.*] Eh! Not bulls. Because bulls give no milk. Eleven cows. They must give a lot of milk. What makes a cow give milk?

54

RICHARD

[*Takes his hand.*] Who knows? Do you understand what it is to give a thing?

ARCHIE

To give? Yes.

RICHARD

While you have a thing it can be taken from you.

ARCHIE

By robbers? No?

RICHARD

But when you give it, you have given it. No robber can take it from you. [*He bends his head and presses his son's hand against his cheek.*] It is yours then for ever when you have given it. It will be yours always. That is to give.

ARCHIE

But, pappie?

RICHARD

Yes?

ARCHIE

How could a robber rob a cow? Everyone would see him. In the night, perhaps.

RICHARD

In the night, yes.

ARCHIE

Are there robbers here like in Rome?

RICHARD

There are poor people everywhere.

ARCHIE

Have they revolvers?

RICHARD

No.

ARCHIE

Knives? Have they knives?

55

RICHARD

[Sternly.] Yes, yes. Knives and revolvers.

ARCHIE

[Disengages himself.] Ask mamma now. She is coming.

RICHARD

[Makes a movement to rise.] I will.

ARCHIE

No, sit there, pappie. You wait and ask her when she comes
back. I won't be here. I'll be in the garden.

RICHARD

[Sinking back again.] Yes. Go.

ARCHIE

[Kisses him swiftly.] Thanks.

[He runs out quickly by the door at the back leading
into the garden. BERTHA enters by the door on the left.
She approaches the table and stands beside it, fingering
the petals of the roses, looking at RICHARD.]

RICHARD

[Watching her.] Well?

BERTHA

[Absently.] Well. He says he likes me.

RICHARD

[Leans his chin on his hand.] You showed him his note?

BERTHA

Yes. I asked him what it meant.

RICHARD

What did he say it meant?

BERTHA

He said I must know. I said I had an idea. Then he told me he
liked me very much. That I was beautiful – and all that.

RICHARD

Since when!

56

BERTHA

[*Again absently.*] Since when – what?

RICHARD

Since when did he say he liked you?

BERTHA

Always, he said. But more since we came back. He said I was like the moon in this lavender dress. [*Looking at him.*] Had you any words with him – about me?

RICHARD

[*Blandly.*] The usual thing. Not about you.

BERTHA

He was very nervous. You saw that?

RICHARD

Yes. I saw it. What else went on?

BERTHA

He asked me to give him my hand.

RICHARD

[*Smiling.*] In marriage?

BERTHA

[*Smiling.*] No, only to hold.

RICHARD

Did you?

BERTHA

Yes. [*Tearing off a few petals.*] Then he caressed my hand and asked would I let him kiss it. I let him.

RICHARD

Well?

BERTHA

Then he asked could he embrace me – even once? ... And then ...

RICHARD

And then?

57

BERTHA

He put his arm round me.

RICHARD

[*Stares at the floor for a moment, then looks at her again.*]
And then?

BERTHA

He said I had beautiful eyes. And asked could he kiss them.
[*With a gesture.*] I said: Do so.

RICHARD

And he did?

BERTHA

Yes. First one and then the other. [*She breaks off suddenly.*]
Tell me, Dick, does all this disturb you? Because I told you I
don't want that. I think you are only pretending you don't
mind. I don't mind.

RICHARD

[*Quietly.*] I know, dear. But I want to find out what he means
or feels just as you do.

BERTHA

[*Points at him.*] Remember, you allowed me to go on, I told
you the whole thing from the beginning.

RICHARD

[*As before.*] I know, dear . . . And then?

BERTHA

He asked for a kiss. I said: *Take it.*

RICHARD

And then?

BERTHA

[*Crumpling a handful of petals.*] He kissed me.

RICHARD

Your mouth?

BERTHA

Once or twice.

RICHARD

Long kisses?

BERTHA

Fairly long. [*Reflects.*] Yes, the last time.

RICHARD

[*Rubs his hands slowly; then.*] With his lips? Or ... the other way?

BERTHA

Yes, the last time.

RICHARD

Did he ask you to kiss him?

BERTHA

He did.

RICHARD

Did you?

BERTHA

[*Hesitates, then looking straight at him.*] I did. I kissed him.

RICHARD

What way?

BERTHA

[*With a shrug.*] O simply.

RICHARD

Were you excited?

BERTHA

Well, you can imagine. [*Frowning suddenly.*] Not much. He has not nice lips ... Still I was excited, of course. But not like with you, Dick.

RICHARD

Was he?

BERTHA

Excited? Yes, I think he was. He sighed. He was dreadfully nervous.

RICHARD

[*Resting his forehead on his hand.*] I see.

BERTHA

[*Crosses towards the lounge and stands near him.*] Are you jealous?

RICHARD

[*As before.*] No.

BERTHA

[*Quietly.*] You are, Dick.

RICHARD

I am not. Jealous of what?

BERTHA

Because he kissed me.

RICHARD

[*Looks up.*] Is that all?

BERTHA

Yes, that's all. Except that he asked me would I meet him.

RICHARD

Out somewhere?

BERTHA

No. In his house.

RICHARD

[*Surprised.*] Over there with his mother, is it?

BERTHA

No, a house he has. He wrote the address for me.

[*She goes to the desk, takes the key from the flower vase, unlocks the drawer and returns to him with the slip of paper.*]

RICHARD

[*Half to himself.*] Our cottage.

BERTHA

[*Hands him the slip.*] Here.

RICHARD

[*Reads it.*] Yes. Our cottage.

Your . . .?

RICHARD

No, his. I call it ours. [*Looking at her.*] The cottage I told you about so often – that we had the two keys for, he and I. It is his now. Where we used to hold our wild nights, talking, drinking, planning – at that time. Wild nights; yes. He and I together. [*He throws the slip on the couch and rises suddenly.*] And sometimes I alone. [*Stares at her.*] But not quite alone. I told you. You remember?

BERTHA

[*Shocked.*] That place?

RICHARD

[*Walks away from her a few paces and stands still, thinking, holding his chin.*] Yes.

BERTHA

[*Taking up the slip again.*] Where is it?

RICHARD

Do you not know?

BERTHA

He told me to take the tram at Lansdowne Road and to ask the man to let me down there. Is it . . . is it a bad place?

RICHARD

O no, cottages. [*He returns to the lounge and sits down.*] What answer did you give?

BERTHA

No answer. He said he would wait.

RICHARD

Tonight?

BERTHA

Every night, he said. Between eight and nine.

RICHARD

And so I am to go tonight to interview – the professor. About the appointment I am to beg for. [*Looking at her.*] The interview is arranged for tonight by him – between eight and nine. Curious, isn't it? The same hour.

BERTHA

Very.

RICHARD

Did he ask you had I any suspicion?

BERTHA

No.

RICHARD

Did he mention my name?

BERTHA

No.

RICHARD

Not once?

BERTHA

Not that I remember.

RICHARD

[*Bounding to his feet.*] O yes! Quite clear!

BERTHA

What?

RICHARD

[*Striding to and fro.*] A liar, a thief, and a fool! Quite clear! A common thief! What else? [*With a harsh laugh.*] My great friend! A patriot too! A thief – nothing else! [*He halts, thrusting his hands into his pockets.*] But a fool also!

BERTHA

[*Looking at him.*] What are you going to do?

RICHARD

[*Shortly.*] Follow him. Find him. Tell him. [*Calmly.*] A few words will do. Thief and fool.

BERTHA

[*Flings the slip on the couch.*] I see it all!

RICHARD

[*Turning.*] Eh!

BERTHA

[*Hotly.*] The work of a devil.

RICHARD

He?

BERTHA

[*Turning on him.*] No, you! The work of a devil to turn him
against me as you tried to turn my own child against me.
Only you did not succeed.

RICHARD

How? In God's name, how?

BERTHA

[*Excitedly.*] Yes, yes. What I say. Everyone saw it. Whenever
I tried to correct him for the least thing you went on with
your folly, speaking to him as if he were a grownup man.
Ruining the poor child, or trying to. Then, of course, I was
the cruel mother and only you loved him. [*With growing
excitement.*] But you did not turn him against me — against
his own mother. Because why? Because the child has too
much nature in him.

RICHARD

I never tried to do such a thing, Bertha. You know I cannot be
severe with a child.

BERTHA

Because you never loved your own mother. A mother is
always a mother, no matter what. I never heard of any
human being that did not love the mother that brought him
into the world, except you.

RICHARD

[*Approaching her quietly.*] Bertha, do not say things you will
be sorry for. Are you not glad my son is fond of me?

BERTHA

Who taught him to be? Who taught him to run to meet you?
Who told him you would bring him home toys when you

were out on your rambles in the rain, forgetting all about him – and me? I did. I taught him to love you.

RICHARD

Yes, dear. I know it was you.

BERTHA

[*Almost crying.*] And then you try to turn everyone against me. All is to be for you. I am to appear false and cruel to everyone except to you. Because you take advantage of my simplicity as you did – the first time.

RICHARD

[*Violently.*] And you have the courage to say that to me?

BERTHA

[*Facing him.*] Yes, I have! Both then and now. Because I am simple you think you can do what you like with me. [*Gesticulating.*] Follow him now. Call him names. Make him be humble before you and make him despise me. Follow him!

RICHARD

[*Controlling himself.*] You forget that I have allowed you complete liberty – and allow you it still.

BERTHA

[*Scornfully.*] Liberty!

RICHARD

Yes, complete. But he must know that I know. [*More calmly.*] I will speak to him quietly. [*Appealing.*] Bertha, believe me, dear! It is not jealousy. You have complete liberty to do as you wish – you and he. But not in this way. He will not despise you. You don't wish to deceive me or to pretend to deceive me – with him, do you?

BERTHA

No, I do not. [*Looking full at him.*] Which of us two is the deceiver?

RICHARD

Of us? You and me?

BERTHA

[*In a calm decided tone.*] I know why you have allowed me
what you call complete liberty.

RICHARD

Why?

BERTHA

To have complete liberty with – that girl.

RICHARD

[*Irritated.*] But, good God, you knew about that this long
time. I never hid it.

BERTHA

You did. I thought it was a kind of friendship between you –
till we came back, and then I saw.

RICHARD

So it is, Bertha.

BERTHA

[*Shakes her head.*] No, no. It is much more; and that is why
you give me complete liberty. All those things you sit up at
night to write about [*pointing to the study*] in there – about
her. You call that friendship?

RICHARD

Believe me, Bertha dear. Believe me as I believe you.

BERTHA

[*With an impulsive gesture.*] My God, I feel it! I know it!
What else is between you but love?

RICHARD

[*Calmly.*] You are trying to put that idea into my head, but I
warn you that I don't take my ideas from other people.

BERTHA

[*Hotly.*] It is, it is! And that is why you allow him to go on.
Of course! It doesn't affect you. You love her.

RICHARD

Love! [*Throws out his hands with a sigh and moves away
from her.*] I cannot argue with you.

BERTHA

You can't because I am right. [*Following him a few steps.*]
What would anyone say?

RICHARD

[*Turns to her.*] Do you think I care?

BERTHA

But I care. What would he say if he knew? You, who talk so
much of the high kind of feeling you have for me, expressing
yourself in that way to another woman. If he did it, or other
men, I could understand because they are false pretenders.
But you, Dick! Why do you not tell him then?

RICHARD

You can if you like.

BERTHA

I will. Certainly I will.

RICHARD

[*Coolly.*] He will explain it to you.

BERTHA

He doesn't say one thing and do another. He is honest in his
own way.

RICHARD

[*Plucks one of the roses and throws it at her feet.*] He is,
indeed! The soul of honour!

BERTHA

You may make fun of him as much as you like. I understand
more than you think about that business. And so will he.
Writing those long letters to her for years, and she to you.
For years. But since I came back I understand it – well.

RICHARD

You do not. Nor would he.

BERTHA

[*Laughs scornfully.*] Of course. Neither he nor I can understand it. Only she can. Because it is such a deep thing!

RICHARD

[*Angrily.*] Neither he nor you – nor she either! Not one of you!

BERTHA

[*With great bitterness.*] She will! She will understand it! The diseased woman!

> [*She turns away and walks over to the little table on the right.* RICHARD *restrains a sudden gesture. A short pause.*]

RICHARD

[*Gravely.*] Bertha, take care of uttering words like that!

BERTHA

[*Turning, excitedly.*] I don't mean any harm! I feel for her more than you can because I am a woman. I do, sincerely. But what I say is true.

RICHARD

Is it generous? Think.

BERTHA

[*Pointing towards the garden.*] It is she who is not generous. Remember now what I say.

RICHARD

What?

BERTHA

[*Comes nearer; in a calmer tone.*] You have given that woman very much, Dick. And she may be worthy of it. And she may understand it all, too. I know she is that kind.

RICHARD

Do you believe that?

BERTHA

I do. But I believe you will get very little from her in return – or from any of her clan. Remember my words, Dick. Because she is not generous and they are not generous. Is it all wrong what I am saying? Is it?

RICHARD

[*Darkly.*] No. Not all.

> [*She stoops and, picking up the rose from the floor,
> places it in the vase again. He watches her.* BRIGID
> *appears at the folding doors on the right.*]

BRIGID

The tea is on the table, ma'am.

BERTHA

Very well.

BRIGID

Is Master Archie in the garden?

BERTHA

Yes. Call him in.

> [BRIGID *crosses the room and goes out into the garden.*
> BERTHA *goes towards the doors on the right. At the
> lounge she stops and takes up the slip.*]

BRIGID

[*In the garden.*] Master Archie! You are to come in to your
tea.

BERTHA

Am I to go to this place?

RICHARD

Do you want to go?

BERTHA

I want to find out what he means. Am I to go?

RICHARD

Why do you ask me? Decide yourself.

BERTHA

Do you tell me to go?

RICHARD

No.

BERTHA

Do you forbid me to go?

RICHARD

No.

BRIGID

[From the garden.] Come quickly, Master Archie! Your tea is waiting on you.

[BRIGID crosses the room and goes out through the folding doors. BERTHA folds the slip into the waist of her dress and goes slowly towards the right. Near the door she turns and halts.]

BERTHA

Tell me not to go and I will not.

RICHARD

[Without looking at her.] Decide yourself.

BERTHA

Will you blame me then?

RICHARD

[Excitedly.] No, no! I will not blame you. You are free. I cannot blame you.

[ARCHIE appears at the garden door.]

BERTHA

I did not deceive you.

[She goes out through the folding doors. RICHARD remains standing at the table. ARCHIE, when his mother has gone, runs down to RICHARD.]

ARCHIE

[Quickly.] Well, did you ask her?

RICHARD

[Starting.] What?

ARCHIE

Can I go?

RICHARD

Yes.

ARCHIE

In the morning? She said yes?

RICHARD

Yes. In the morning.

[*He puts his arm round his son's shoulders and looks down at him fondly.*]

SECOND ACT

A room in Robert Hand's cottage at Ranelagh. On the right, forward, a small black piano, on the rest of which is an open piece of music. Farther back a door leading to the street door. In the wall, at the back, folding doors, draped with dark curtains, leading to a bedroom. Near the piano a large table, on which is a tall oil lamp with a wide yellow shade. Chairs, upholstered, near this table. A small cardtable more forward. Against the back wall a bookcase. In the left wall, back, a window looking out into the garden, and, forward, a door and porch, also leading to the garden. Easychairs here and there. Plants in the porch and near the draped folding doors. On the walls are many framed black and white designs. In the right corner, back, a sideboard; and in the centre of the room, left of the table, a group consisting of a standing Turkish pipe, a low oil stove, which is not lit, and a rocking-chair. It is the evening of the same day.

> [ROBERT HAND, in evening dress, is seated at the piano. The candles are not lit but the lamp on the table is lit. He plays softly in the bass the first bars of Wolfram's song in the last act of 'Tannhäuser'. Then he breaks off and, resting an elbow on the ledge of the keyboard, meditates. Then he rises and, pulling out a pump from behind the piano, walks here and there in the room ejecting from it into the air sprays of perfume. He inhales the air slowly and then puts the pump back behind the piano. He sits down on a chair near the table and, smoothing his hair carefully, sighs once or twice. Then, thrusting his hands into his trousers pockets, he leans back, stretches out his legs, and waits. A knock is heard at the street door. He rises quickly.]

ROBERT

[Exclaims.] Bertha!

> [He hurries out by the door on the right. There is a noise

of confused greeting. After a few moments ROBERT
enters, followed by RICHARD ROWAN, *who is in grey
tweeds as before but holds in one hand a dark felt hat
and in the other an umbrella.*]

ROBERT

First of all let me put these outside.

[*He takes the hat and umbrella, leaves them in the hall
and returns.*]

ROBERT

[*Pulling round a chair.*] Here you are. You are lucky to find
me in. Why didn't you tell me today? You were always a
devil for surprises. I suppose my evocation of the past was too
much for your wild blood. See how artistic I have become.
[*He points to the walls.*] The piano is an addition since your
time. I was just strumming out Wagner when you came.
Killing time. You see I am ready for the fray. [*Laughs.*] I was
just wondering how you and the vicechancellor were getting
on together. [*With exaggerated alarm.*] But are you going in
that suit? O well, it doesn't make much odds, I suppose. But
how goes the time? [*He takes out his watch.*] Twenty past
eight already, I declare!

RICHARD

Have you an appointment?

ROBERT

[*Laughs nervously.*] Suspicious to the last!

RICHARD

Then I may sit down?

ROBERT

Of course, of course. [*They both sit down.*] For a few minutes,
anyhow. Then we can both go on together. We are not bound
for time. Between eight and nine, he said, didn't he? What
time is it, I wonder? [*Is about to look again at his watch; then
stops.*] Twenty past eight, yes.

RICHARD

[*Wearily, sadly.*] Your appointment also was for the same
hour. Here.

72

ROBERT

What appointment?

RICHARD

With Bertha.

ROBERT

[*Stares at him.*] Are you mad?

RICHARD

Are you?

ROBERT

[*After a long pause.*] Who told you?

RICHARD

She.

[*A short silence.*]

ROBERT

[*In a low voice.*] Yes. I must have been mad. *Rapidly.* Listen to me, Richard. It is a great relief to me that you have come – the greatest relief. I assure you that ever since this afternoon I have thought and thought how I could break it off without seeming a fool. A great relief! I even intended to send word ... a letter, a few lines. [*Suddenly.*] But then it was too late ... [*Passes his hand over his forehead.*] Let me speak frankly with you; let me tell you everything.

RICHARD

I know everything. I have known for some time.

ROBERT

Since when?

RICHARD

Since it began between you and her.

ROBERT

[*Again rapidly.*] Yes, I was mad. But it was merely light-headedness. I admit that to have asked her here this evening was a mistake. I can explain everything to you. And I will. Truly.

73

Explain to me what is the word you longed and never dared
to say to her. If you can or will.

ROBERT

[*Looks down, then raises his head.*] Yes. I will. I admire very
much the personality of your ... of ... your wife. That is
the word. I can say it. It is no secret.

RICHARD

Then why did you wish to keep secret your wooing?

ROBERT

Wooing?

RICHARD

Your advances to her, little by little, day after day, looks,
whispers. [*With a nervous movement of the hands.*] In-
somma, wooing.

ROBERT

[*Bewildered.*] But how do you know all this?

RICHARD

She told me.

ROBERT

This afternoon?

RICHARD

No. Time after time, as it happened.

ROBERT

You knew? From her? [RICHARD *nods.*] You were watching
us all the time?

RICHARD

[*Very coldly.*] I was watching you.

ROBERT

[*Quickly.*] I mean, watching me. And you never spoke! You
had only to speak a word – to save me from myself. You were
trying me. [*Passes his hand again over his forehead.*] It was a
terrible trial: now also. [*Desperately.*] Well, it is past. It will

74

be a lesson to me for all my life. You hate me now for what I have done and for . . .

RICHARD

[*Quietly, looking at him.*] Have I said that I hate you?

ROBERT

Do you not? You must.

RICHARD

Even if Bertha had not told me I should have known. Did you not see that when I came in this afternoon I went into my study suddenly for a moment?

ROBERT

You did. I remember.

RICHARD

To give you time to recover yourself. It made me sad to see your eyes. And the roses too. I cannot say why. A great mass of overblown roses.

ROBERT

I thought I had to give them. Was that strange? [*Looks at* RICHARD *with a tortured expression.*] Too many, perhaps? Or too old or common?

RICHARD

That was why I did not hate you. The whole thing made me sad all at once.

ROBERT

[*To himself.*] And this is real. It is happening – to us.

[*He stares before him for some moments in silence, as if dazed; then, without turning his head, continues.*]

ROBERT

And she, too, was trying me; making an experiment with me for your sake!

RICHARD

You know women better than I do. She says she felt pity for you.

75

ROBERT

[*Brooding.*] Pitied me, because I am no longer ... an ideal lover. Like my roses. Common, old.

RICHARD

Like all men you have a foolish wandering heart.

ROBERT

[*Slowly.*] Well, you spoke at last. You chose the right moment.

RICHARD

[*Leans forward.*] Robert, not like this. For us two, no. Years, a whole life, of friendship. Think a moment. Since childhood, boyhood ... No, no. Not in such a way – like thieves – at night. [*Glancing about him.*] And in such a place. No, Robert, that is not for people like us.

ROBERT

What a lesson! Richard, I cannot tell you what a relief it is to me that you have spoken – that the danger is passed. Yes, yes. [*Somewhat diffidently.*] Because ... there was some danger for you, too, if you think. Was there not?

RICHARD

What danger?

ROBERT

[*In the same tone.*] I don't know. I mean if you had not spoken. If you had watched and waited on until ...

RICHARD

Until?

ROBERT

[*Bravely.*] Until I had come to like her more and more (because I can assure you it is only a lightheaded idea of mine), to like her deeply, to love her. Would you have spoken to me then as you have just now? [RICHARD *is silent.* ROBERT *goes on more boldly.*] It would have been different, would it not? For then it might have been too late while it is not too late now. What could I have said then? I could have said only: 'You are my friend, my dear good friend. I am very sorry but

76

I love her. [*With a sudden fervent gesture.*] I love her and I will take her from you, however I can, because I love her.

[*They look at each other for some moments in silence.*]

RICHARD

[*Calmly.*] That is the language I have heard often and never believed in. Do you mean by stealth or by violence? Steal you could not in my house because the doors were open; nor take by violence if there were no resistance.

ROBERT

You forget that the kingdom of heaven suffers violence: and the kingdom of heaven is like a woman.

RICHARD

[*Smiling.*] Go on.

ROBERT

[*Diffidently, but bravely.*] Do you think you have rights over her – over her heart?

RICHARD

None.

ROBERT

For what you have done for her? So much! You claim nothing?

RICHARD

Nothing.

ROBERT

[*After a pause strikes his forehead with his hand.*] What am I saying? Or what am I thinking? I wish you would upbraid me, curse me, hate me as I deserve. You love this woman. I remember all you told me long ago. She is yours, your work. [*Suddenly.*] And that is why I, too, was drawn to her. You are so strong that you attract me even through her.

RICHARD

I am weak.

ROBERT

[*With enthusiasm.*] You, Richard! You are the incarnation of strength.

RICHARD
[*Holds out his hands.*] Feel those hands.

ROBERT
[*Taking his hands.*] Yes. Mine are stronger. But I meant strength of another kind.

RICHARD
[*Gloomily.*] I think you would try to take her by violence.

[*He withdraws his hands slowly.*]

ROBERT
[*Rapidly.*] Those are moments of sheer madness when we feel an intense passion for a woman. We see nothing. We think of nothing. Only to possess her. Call it brutal, bestial, what you will.

RICHARD
[*A little timidly.*] I am afraid that that longing to possess a woman is not love.

ROBERT
[*Impatiently.*] No man ever yet lived on this earth who did not long to possess — I mean to possess in the flesh — the woman whom he loves. It is nature's law.

RICHARD
[*Contemptuously.*] What is that to me? Did I vote it?

ROBERT
But if you love . . . What else is it?

RICHARD
[*Hesitatingly.*] To wish her well.

ROBERT
[*Warmly.*] But the passion which burns us night and day to possess her. You feel it as I do. And it is not what you said now.

RICHARD
Have you . . .? [*He stops for an instant.*] Have you the luminous certitude that yours is the brain in contact with which she must think and understand and that yours is the body in contact with which her body must feel? Have you this certitude in yourself?

ROBERT

Have you?

RICHARD

[*Moved.*] Once I had it, Robert: a certitude as luminous as that of my own existence – or an illusion as luminous.

ROBERT

[*Cautiously.*] And now?

RICHARD

If you had it and I could feel that you had it – even now ...

ROBERT

What would you do?

RICHARD

[*Quietly.*] Go away. You, and not I, would be necessary to her. Alone as I was before I met her.

ROBERT

[*Rubs his hands nervously.*] A nice little load on my conscience!

RICHARD

[*Abstractedly.*] You met my son when you came to my house this afternoon. He told me. What did you feel?

ROBERT

[*Promptly.*] Pleasure.

RICHARD

Nothing else?

ROBERT

Nothing else. Unless I thought of two things at the same time. I am like that. If my best friend lay in his coffin and his face had a comic expression I should smile. [*With a little gesture of despair.*] I am like that. But I should suffer too, deeply.

RICHARD

You spoke of conscience ... Did he seem to you a child only – or an angel?

79

ROBERT

[*Shakes his head.*] No. Neither an angel nor an Anglo-Saxon. Two things, by the way, for which I have very little sympathy.

RICHARD

Never then? Never even ... with her? Tell me. I wish to know.

ROBERT

I feel in my heart something different. I believe that on the last day (if it ever comes), when we are all assembled together, that the Almighty will speak to us like this. We will say that we lived chastely with one other creature ...

RICHARD

[*Bitterly.*] Lie to Him?

ROBERT

Or that we tried to. And He will say to us: Fools! Who told you that you were to give yourselves to one being only? You were made to give yourself to many freely. I wrote that law with My finger on your hearts.

RICHARD

On woman's heart, too?

ROBERT

Yes. Can we close our heart against an affection which we feel deeply? Should we close it? Should she?

RICHARD

We are speaking of bodily union.

ROBERT

Affection between man and woman must come to that. We think too much of it because our minds are warped. For us today it is of no more consequence than any other form of contact – than a kiss.

RICHARD

If it is of no consequence why are you dissatisfied till you reach that end? Why were you waiting here tonight?

Passion tends to go as far as it can; but, you may believe me or not, I had not that in my mind – to reach that end.

RICHARD

Reach it if you can. I will use no arm against you that the world puts in my hand. If the law which God's finger has written on our hearts is the law you say I too am God's creature.

[*He rises and paces to and fro some moments in silence. Then he goes towards the porch and leans against the jamb.* ROBERT *watches him.*]

ROBERT

I always felt it. In myself and in others.

RICHARD

[*Absently.*] Yes?

ROBERT

[*With a vague gesture.*] For all. That a woman, too, has the right to try with many men until she finds love. An immoral idea, is it not? I wanted to write a book about it. I began it . . .

RICHARD

[*As before.*] Yes?

ROBERT

Because I knew a woman who seemed to me to be doing that – carrying out that idea in her own life. She interested me very much.

RICHARD

When was this?

ROBERT

O, not lately. When you were away.

[RICHARD *leaves his place rather abruptly and again paces to and fro.*]

ROBERT

You see, I am more honest than you thought.

RICHARD

I wish you had not thought of her now – whoever she was, or is.

ROBERT

[*Easily.*] She was and is the wife of a stockbroker.

RICHARD

[*Turning.*] You know him?

ROBERT

Intimately.

[RICHARD *sits down again in the same place and leans forward, his head on his hands.*]

ROBERT

[*Moving his chair a little closer.*] May I ask you a question?

RICHARD

You may.

ROBERT

[*With some hesitation.*] Has it never happened to you in these years – I mean when you were away from her, perhaps, or travelling – to ... betray her with another. Betray her, I mean, not in love. Carnally, I mean ... Has that never happened?

RICHARD

It has.

ROBERT

And what did you do?

RICHARD

[*As before.*] I remember the first time. I came home. It was night. My house was silent. My little son was sleeping in his cot. She, too, was asleep. I wakened her from sleep and told her. I cried beside her bed; and I pierced her heart.

ROBERT

O, Richard, why did you do that?

RICHARD

Betray her?

ROBERT

No. But tell her, waken her from sleep to tell her. It was piercing her heart.

RICHARD

She must know me as I am.

ROBERT

But that is not you as you are. A moment of weakness.

RICHARD

[*Lost in thought.*] And I was feeding the flame of her innocence with my guilt.

ROBERT

[*Brusquely.*] O, don't talk of guilt and innocence. You have made her all that she is. A strange and wonderful personality – in my eyes, at least.

RICHARD

[*Darkly.*] Or I have killed her.

ROBERT

Killed her?

RICHARD

The virginity of her soul.

ROBERT

[*Impatiently.*] Well lost! What would she be without you?

RICHARD

I tried to give her a new life.

ROBERT

And you have. A new and rich life.

RICHARD

Is it worth what I have taken from her – her girlhood, her laughter, her young beauty, the hopes in her young heart?

ROBERT

[*Firmly.*] Yes. Well worth it. [*He looks at* RICHARD *for some moments in silence.*] If you had neglected her, lived wildly, brought her away so far only to make her suffer . . .

[*He stops.* RICHARD *raises his head and looks at him.*]

RICHARD

If I had?

ROBERT

[*Slightly confused.*] You know there were rumours here of your life abroad – a wild life. Some persons who knew you or met you or heard of you in Rome. Lying rumours.

RICHARD

[*Coldly.*] Continue.

ROBERT

[*Laughs a little harshly.*] Even I at times thought of her as a victim. [*Smoothly.*] And of course, Richard, I felt and knew all the time that you were a man of great talent – of something more than talent. And that was your excuse – a valid one in my eyes.

RICHARD

Have you thought that it is perhaps now – at this moment – that I am neglecting her? [*He clasps his hands nervously and leans across towards* ROBERT.] I may be silent still. And she may yield to you at last – wholly and many times.

ROBERT

[*Draws back at once.*] My dear Richard, my dear friend, I swear to you I could not make you suffer.

RICHARD

[*Continuing.*] You may then know in soul and body, in a hundred forms, and ever restlessly, what some old theologian, Duns Scotus, I think, called a death of the spirit.

ROBERT

[*Eagerly.*] A death. No; its affirmation! A death! The supreme instant of life from which all coming life proceeds, the eternal law of nature herself.

RICHARD

And that other law of nature, as you call it: change. How will it be when you turn against her and against me; when her beauty, or what seems so to you now, wearies you and my affection for you seems false and odious?

ROBERT

That will never be. Never.

RICHARD

And you turn even against yourself for having known me or trafficked with us both?

ROBERT

[*Gravely.*] It will never be like that, Richard. Be sure of that.

RICHARD

[*Contemptuously.*] I care very little whether it is or not because there is something I fear much more.

ROBERT

[*Shakes his head.*] You fear? I disbelieve you, Richard. Since we were boys together I have followed your mind. You do not know what moral fear is.

RICHARD

[*Lays his hand on his arm.*] Listen. She is dead. She lies on my bed. I look at her body which I betrayed – grossly and many times. And loved, too, and wept over. And I know that her body was always my loyal slave. To me, to me only she gave ... [*He breaks off and turns aside, unable to speak.*]

ROBERT

[*Softly.*] Do not suffer, Richard. There is no need. She is loyal to you, body and soul. Why do you fear?

RICHARD

[*Turns towards him, almost fiercely.*] Not that fear. But that I will reproach myself then for having taken all for myself because I would not suffer her to give to another what was hers and not mine to give, because I accepted from her her loyalty and made her life poorer in love. That is my fear. That I stand between her and any moments of life that

85

should be hers, between her and you, between her and any-one, between her and anything. I will not do it. I cannot and I will not. I dare not.

[*He leans back in his chair breathless, with shining eyes.* ROBERT *rises quietly, and stands behind his chair.*]

ROBERT

Look here, Richard. We have said all there is to be said. Let the past be past.

RICHARD

[*Quickly and harshly.*] Wait. One thing more. For you, too, must know me as I am – now.

ROBERT

More? Is there more?

RICHARD

I told you that when I saw your eyes this afternoon I felt sad. Your humility and confusion, I felt, united you to me in brotherhood. [*He turns half round towards him.*] At that moment I felt our whole life together in the past, and I longed to put my arm around your neck.

ROBERT

[*Deeply and suddenly touched.*] It is noble of you, Richard, to forgive me like this.

RICHARD

[*Struggling with himself.*] I told you that I wished you not to do anything false and secret against me – against our friend-ship, against her; not to steal from me, craftily, secretly, meanly – in the dark, in the night – you, Robert, my friend.

ROBERT

I know. And it was noble of you.

RICHARD

[*Looks up at him with a steady gaze.*] No. Not noble. Ignoble.

ROBERT

[*Makes an involuntary gesture.*] How? Why?

RICHARD

[*Looks away again; in a lower voice.*] That is what I must tell you too. Because in the very core of my ignoble heart I longed to be betrayed by you and by her – in the dark, in the night – secretly, meanly, craftily. By you, my best friend, and by her. I longed for that passionately and ignobly, to be dishonoured for ever in love and in lust, to be . . .

ROBERT

[*Bending down, places his hands over* RICHARD's *mouth.*] Enough. Enough. [*He takes his hands away.*] But no. Go on.

RICHARD

To be for ever a shameful creature and to build up my soul again out of the ruins of its shame.

ROBERT

And that is why you wished that she . . .

RICHARD

[*With calm.*] She has spoken always of her innocence, as I have spoken always of my guilt, humbling me.

ROBERT

From pride, then?

RICHARD

From pride and from ignoble longing. And from a motive deeper still.

ROBERT

[*With decision.*] I understand you.

[*He returns to his place and begins to speak at once, drawing his chair closer.*]

ROBERT

May it not be that we are here and now in the presence of a moment which will free us both – me as well as you – from the last bonds of what is called morality. My friendship for you has laid bonds on me.

RICHARD

Light bonds, apparently.

ROBERT

I acted in the dark, secretly. I will do so no longer. Have you the courage to allow me to act freely?

RICHARD

A duel – between us?

ROBERT

[*With growing excitement.*] A battle of both our souls, different as they are, against all that is false in them and in the world. A battle of your soul against the spectre of fidelity, of mine against the spectre of friendship. All life is a conquest, the victory of human passion over the commandments of cowardice. Will, you, Richard? Have you the courage? Even if it shatters to atoms the friendship between us, even if it breaks up for ever the last illusion in your own life? There was an eternity before we were born: another will come after we are dead. The blinding instant of passion alone – passion, free, unashamed, irresistible – that is the only gate by which we can escape from the misery of what slaves call life. Is not this the language of your own youth that I heard so often from you in this very place where we are sitting now? Have you changed?

RICHARD

[*Passes his hand across his brow.*] Yes. It is the language of my youth.

ROBERT

[*Eagerly, intensely.*] Richard, you have driven me up to this point. She and I have only obeyed your will. You yourself have roused these words in my brain. Your own words. Shall we? Freely? Together?

RICHARD

[*Mastering his emotion.*] Together no. Fight your part alone. I will not free you. Leave me to fight mine.

ROBERT

[*Rises, decided.*] You allow me, then?

RICHARD

[*Rises also, calmly.*] Free yourself.

[*A knock is heard at the hall door.*]

ROBERT

[*In alarm.*] What does this mean?

RICHARD

[*Calmly.*] Bertha, evidently. Did you not ask her to come?

ROBERT

Yes, but ... [*Looking about him.*] Then I am going, Richard.

RICHARD

No. I am going.

ROBERT

[*Desperately.*] Richard, I appeal to you. Let me go. It is over. She is yours. Keep her and forgive me, both of you.

RICHARD

Because you are generous enough to allow me?

ROBERT

[*Hotly.*] Richard, you will make me angry with you if you say that.

RICHARD

Angry or not, I will not live on your generosity. You have asked her to meet you here tonight and alone. Solve the question between you.

ROBERT

[*Promptly.*] Open the door. I shall wait in the garden. [*He goes towards the porch.*] Explain to her, Richard, as best you can. I cannot see her now.

RICHARD

I shall go, I tell you. Wait out there if you wish.

[*He goes out by the door on the right.* ROBERT *goes out hastily through the porch but comes back the same instant.*]

ROBERT

An umbrella! [*With a sudden gesture.*] O!

[*He goes out again through the porch. The hall door is heard to open and close.* RICHARD *enters, followed by* BERTHA, *who is dressed in a dark-brown costume and wears a small dark red hat. She has neither umbrella nor waterproof.*]

RICHARD

[*Gaily.*] Welcome back to old Ireland!

BERTHA

[*Nervously, seriously.*] Is this the place?

RICHARD

Yes, it is. How did you find it?

BERTHA

I told the cabman. I didn't like to ask my way. [*Looking about her curiously.*] Was he not waiting? He has gone away?

RICHARD

[*Points towards the garden.*] He is waiting. Out there. He was waiting when I came.

BERTHA

[*Selfpossessed again.*] You see, you came after all.

RICHARD

Did you think I would not?

BERTHA

I knew you could not remain away. You see, after all you are like all other men. You had to come. You are jealous like the others.

RICHARD

You seem annoyed to find me here.

BERTHA

What happened between you?

RICHARD

I told him I knew everything, that I had known for a long time. He asked how. I said from you.

BERTHA

Does he hate me?

RICHARD

I cannot read in his heart.

BERTHA

[*Sits down helplessly.*] Yes. He hates me. He believes I made a fool of him – betrayed him. I knew he would.

RICHARD

I told him you were sincere with him.

BERTHA

He does not believe it. Nobody would believe it. I should have told him first – not you.

RICHARD

I thought he was a common robber, prepared to use even violence against you. I had to protect you from that.

BERTHA

That I could have done myself.

RICHARD

Are you sure?

BERTHA

It would have been enough to have told him that you knew I was here. Now I can find out nothing. He hates me. He is right to hate me. I have treated him badly, shamefully.

RICHARD

[*Takes her hand.*] Bertha, look at me.

BERTHA

[*Turns to him.*] Well?

RICHARD

[*Gazes into her eyes and then lets her hand fall.*] I cannot read in your heart either.

BERTHA

[*Still looking at him.*] You could not remain away. Do you not trust me? You can see I am quite calm. I could have hidden it all from you.

RICHARD

I doubt that.

BERTHA

[*With a slight toss of her head.*] O, easily if I had wanted to.

RICHARD

[*Darkly.*] Perhaps you are sorry now that you did not.

BERTHA

Perhaps I am.

RICHARD

[*Unpleasantly.*] What a fool you were to tell me! It would have been so nice if you had kept it secret.

BERTHA

As you do, no?

RICHARD

As I do, yes. [*He turns to go.*] Goodbye for a while.

BERTHA

[*Alarmed, rises.*] Are you going?

RICHARD

Naturally. My part is ended here.

BERTHA

To her, I suppose?

RICHARD

[*Astonished.*] Who?

BERTHA

Her ladyship. I suppose it is all planned so that you may have a good opportunity. To meet her and have an intellectual conversation!

RICHARD

[*With an outburst of rude anger.*] To meet the devil's father!

BERTHA

[*Unpins her hat and sits down.*] Very well. You can go. Now I know what to do.

RICHARD

[*Returns, approaches her.*] You don't believe a word of what
you say.

BERTHA

[*Calmly.*] You can go. Why don't you?

RICHARD

Then you have come here and led him on in this way on
account of me. Is that how it is?

BERTHA

There is one person in all this who is not a fool. And that is
you. I am though. And he is.

RICHARD

[*Continuing.*] If so you have indeed treated him badly and
shamefully.

BERTHA

[*Points at him.*] Yes. But it was your fault. And I will end it
now. I am simply a tool for you. You have no respect for me.
You never had because I did what I did.

RICHARD

And has he respect?

BERTHA

He has. Of all the persons I met since I came back he is the
only one who has. And he knows what they only suspect.
And that is why I liked him from the first and like him still.
Great respect for me she has! Why did you not ask her to
come away with you nine years ago?

RICHARD

You know why, Bertha. Ask yourself.

BERTHA

Yes, I know why. You knew the answer you would get. That
is why.

RICHARD

That is not why. I did not even ask you.

Yes. You knew I would go, asked or not. I do things. But if I
do one thing I can do two things. As I have the name I can
have the gains.

RICHARD

[*With increasing excitement.*] Bertha, I accept what is to be. I
have trusted you. I will trust you still.

BERTHA

To have that against me. To leave me then. [*Almost passionately.*] Why do you not defend me then against him? Why do
you go away from me now without a word? Dick, my God,
tell me what you wish me to do?

RICHARD

I cannot, dear [*Struggling with himself.*] Your own heart will
tell you. [*He seizes both her hands.*] I have a wild delight in
my soul, Bertha, as I look at you. I see you as you are yourself. That I came first in your life or before him then – that
may be nothing to you. You may be his more than mine.

BERTHA

I am not. Only I feel for him too.

RICHARD

And I do too. You may be his and mine. I will trust you,
Bertha, and him too. I must. I cannot hate him since his arms
have been around you. You have drawn us near together.
There is something wiser than wisdom in your heart. Who
am I that I should call myself master of your heart or of any
woman's? Bertha, love him, be his, give yourself to him if you
desire – or if you can.

BERTHA

[*Dreamily.*] I will remain.

RICHARD

Goodbye.

[*He lets her hand fall and goes out rapidly on the right.*
BERTHA *remains sitting. Then she rises and goes timidly
towards the porch. She stops near it and, after a little
hesitation, calls into the garden.*]

Is anyone out there?

[*At the same time she retreats towards the middle of the room. Then she calls again in the same way.*]

Is anyone there?

[ROBERT *appears in the open doorway that leads in from the garden. His coat is buttoned and the collar is turned up. He holds the doorposts with his hands lightly and waits for* BERTHA *to see him.*]

[*Catching sight of him, starts back: then, quickly.*] Robert!

Are you alone?

Yes.

[*Looking towards the door on the right.*] Where is he?

Gone. [*Nervously.*] You startled me. Where did you come from?

[*With a movement of his head.*] Out there. Did he not tell you I was out there – waiting?

[*Quickly.*] Yes, he told me. But I was afraid here alone. With the door open, waiting. [*She comes to the table and rests her hand on the corner.*] Why do you stand like that in the doorway?

Why? I am afraid too.

Of what?

ROBERT

Of you.

BERTHA

[Looks down.] Do you hate me now?

ROBERT

I fear you. [Clasping his hands at his back, quietly but a little defiantly.] I fear a new torture – a new trap.

BERTHA

[As before.] For what do you blame me?

ROBERT

[Comes forward a few steps, halts: then impulsively.] Why did you lead me on? Day after day, more and more. Why did you not stop me? You could have – with a word. But not even a word! I forgot myself and him. You saw it. That I was ruining myself in his eyes, losing his friendship. Did you want me to?

BERTHA

[Looking up.] You never asked me.

ROBERT

Asked you what?

BERTHA

If he suspected – or knew.

ROBERT

And would you have told me?

BERTHA

Yes.

ROBERT

[Hesitatingly.] Did you tell him – everything?

BERTHA

I did.

ROBERT

I mean – details.

BERTHA

Everything.

ROBERT

[*With a forced smile.*] I see. You were making an experiment for his sake. On me. Well, why not? It seems I was a good subject. Still, it was a little cruel of you.

BERTHA

Try to understand me, Robert. You must try.

ROBERT

[*With a polite gesture.*] Well, I will try.

BERTHA

Why do you stand like that near the door? It makes me nervous to look at you.

ROBERT

I am trying to understand. And then I am afraid.

BERTHA

[*Holds out her hand.*] You need not be afraid.

[ROBERT *comes towards her quickly and takes her hand.*]

ROBERT

[*Diffidently.*] Used you to laugh over me – together? [*Drawing his hand away.*] But now I must be good or you may laugh over me again – tonight.

BERTHA

[*Distressed, lays her hand on his arm.*] Please listen to me, Robert ... But you are all wet, drenched! [*She passes her hand over his coat.*] O, you poor fellow! Out there in the rain all that time! I forgot that.

ROBERT

[*Laughs.*] Yes, you forgot the climate.

BERTHA

But you are really drenched. You must change your coat.

ROBERT

[*Takes her hands.*] Tell me, it is pity then that you feel for me, as he – as Richard – says?

BERTHA

Please change your coat, Robert, when I ask you. You might get a very bad cold from that. Do, please.

ROBERT

What would it matter now?

BERTHA

[*Looking round her.*] Where do you keep your clothes here?

ROBERT

[*Points to the door at the back.*] In there. I fancy I have a jacket here. [*Maliciously.*] In my bedroom.

BERTHA

Well, go in and take that off.

ROBERT

And you?

BERTHA

I will wait here for you.

ROBERT

Do you command me to?

BERTHA

[*Laughing.*] Yes, I command you.

ROBERT

[*Promptly.*] Then I will. [*He goes quickly towards the bedroom door; then turns round.*] You won't go away?

BERTHA

No, I will wait. But don't be long.

ROBERT

Only a moment.

[*He goes into the bedroom, leaving the door open.* BERTHA *looks curiously about her and then glances in indecision towards the door at the back.*]

ROBERT

[*From the bedroom.*] You have not gone?

BERTHA

No.

ROBERT

I am in the dark here. I must light the lamp.

[*He is heard striking a match, and putting a glass shade on a lamp. A pink light comes in through the doorway.* BERTHA *glances at her watch at her wristlet and then sits at the table.*]

ROBERT

[*As before.*] Do you like the effect of the light?

BERTHA

O, yes.

ROBERT

Can you admire it from where you are?

BERTHA

Yes, quite well.

ROBERT

It was for you.

BERTHA

[*Confused.*] I am not worthy even of that.

ROBERT

[*Clearly, harshly.*] Love's labour lost.

BERTHA

[*Rising nervously.*] Robert!

ROBERT

Yes?

BERTHA

Come here, quickly! Quickly, I say!

ROBERT

I am ready.

99

[*He appears in the doorway, wearing a darkgreen velvet jacket. Seeing her agitation, he comes quickly towards her.*]

ROBERT

What is it, Bertha?

BERTHA

[*Trembling.*] I was afraid.

ROBERT

Of being alone?

BERTHA

[*Catches his hands.*] You know what I mean. My nerves are all upset.

ROBERT

That I . . .?

BERTHA

Promise me, Robert, not to think of such a thing. Never. If you like me at all. I thought that moment . . .

ROBERT

What an idea?

BERTHA

But promise me if you like me.

ROBERT

If I like you, Bertha! I promise. Of course, I promise. You are trembling all over.

BERTHA

Let me sit down somewhere. It will pass in a moment.

ROBERT

My poor Bertha! Sit down. Come.

[*He leads her towards a chair near the table. She sits down. He stands beside her.*]

ROBERT

[*After a short pause.*] Has it passed?

BERTHA

Yes. It was only a moment. I was very silly. I was afraid that
... I wanted to see you near me.

ROBERT

That ... that you made me promise not to think of?

BERTHA

Yes.

ROBERT

[*Keenly.*] Or something else?

BERTHA

[*Helplessly.*] Robert, I feared something. I am not sure what.

ROBERT

And now?

BERTHA

Now you are here. I can see you. Now it has passed.

ROBERT

[*With resignation.*] Passed. Yes. Love's labour lost.

BERTHA

[*Looks up at him.*] Listen, Robert. I want to explain to you
about that. I could not deceive Dick. Never. In nothing. I told
him everything – from the first. Then it went on and on: and
still you never spoke or asked me. I wanted you to.

ROBERT

Is that the truth, Bertha?

BERTHA

Yes, because it annoyed me that you could think I was like
... like the other women I suppose you knew that way. I
think that Dick is right too. Why should there be secrets?

ROBERT

[*Softly.*] Still, secrets can be very sweet. Can they not?

BERTHA

[*Smiles.*] Yes, I know they can. But, you see, I could not keep
things secret from Dick. Besides, what is the good? They

always come out in the end. Is it not better for people to
know?

ROBERT

[*Softly and a little shyly.*] How could you, Bertha, tell him
everything? Did you? Every single thing that passed between
us?

BERTHA

Yes. Everything he asked me.

ROBERT

Did he ask you – much?

BERTHA

You know the kind he is. He asks about everything. The ins
and outs.

ROBERT

About our kissing, too?

BERTHA

Of course. I told him all.

ROBERT

[*Shakes his head slowly.*] Extraordinary little person! Were
you not ashamed?

BERTHA

No.

ROBERT

Not a bit?

BERTHA

No. Why? Is that terrible?

ROBERT

And how did he take it? Tell me. I want to know everything,
too.

BERTHA

[*Laughs.*] It excited him. More than usual.

ROBERT

Why? Is he excitable – still?

BERTHA

[*Archly.*] Yes, very. When he is not lost in his philosophy.

ROBERT

More than I?

BERTHA

More than you? [*Reflecting.*] How could I answer that? You both are, I suppose?

[ROBERT *turns aside and gazes towards the porch, passing his hand once or twice thoughtfully over his hair.*]

BERTHA

[*Gently.*] Are you angry with me again?

ROBERT

[*Moodily.*] You are with me.

BERTHA

No, Robert. Why should I be?

ROBERT

Because I asked you to come to this place. I tried to prepare it for you. [*He points vaguely here and there.*] A sense of quietness.

BERTHA

[*Touching his jacket with her fingers.*] And this, too. Your nice velvet coat.

ROBERT

Also. I will keep no secrets from you.

BERTHA

You remind me of someone in a picture. I like you in it ... But you are not angry, are you?

ROBERT

[*Darkly.*] Yes. That was my mistake. To ask you to come here. I felt it when I looked at you from the garden and saw you – you, Bertha – standing here. [*Hopelessly.*] But what else could I have done?

BERTHA

[*Quietly.*] You mean because others have been here?

ROBERT

Yes.

> [*He walks away from her a few paces. A gust of wind makes the lamp on the table flicker. He lowers the wick slightly.*]

BERTHA

[*Following him with her eyes.*] But I knew that before I came. I am not angry with you for it.

ROBERT

[*Shrugs his shoulders.*] Why should you be angry with me after all? You are not even angry with him – for the same thing – or worse.

BERTHA

Did he tell you about himself?

ROBERT

Yes. He told me. We all confess to one another here. Turn about.

BERTHA

I try to forget it.

ROBERT

It does not trouble you?

BERTHA

Not now. Only I dislike to think of it.

ROBERT

It is merely something brutal, you think? of little importance?

BERTHA

It does not trouble me – now.

ROBERT

[*Looking at her over his shoulder.*] But there is something that would trouble you very much and that you would not try to forget?

BERTHA

What?

ROBERT

[*Turning towards her.*] If it were not only something brutal with this person or that – for a few moments. If it were something fine and spiritual – with one person only – with one woman. [*Smiles.*] And perhaps brutal too. It usually comes to that sooner or later. Would you try to forget and forgive that?

BERTHA

[*Toying with her wristlet.*] In whom?

ROBERT

In anyone. In me.

BERTHA

[*Calmly.*] You mean in Dick.

ROBERT

I said in myself. But would you?

BERTHA

You think I would revenge myself? Is Dick not to be free too?

ROBERT

[*Points at her.*] That is not from your heart, Bertha.

BERTHA

[*Proudly.*] Yes, it is; let him be free too. He leaves me free also.

ROBERT

[*Insistently.*] And you know why? And understand? And you like it? And you want to be? And it makes you happy? And has made you happy? Always? This gift of freedom which he gave you – nine years ago?

BERTHA

[*Gazing at him with wide open eyes.*] But why do you ask me such a lot of questions, Robert?

ROBERT

[*Stretches out both hands to her.*] Because I had another gift to offer you then – a common simple gift – like myself. If you want to know it I will tell you.

BERTHA

[*Looking at her watch.*] Past is past, Robert. And I think I ought to go now. It is nine almost.

ROBERT

[*Impetuously.*] No, no. Not yet. There is one confession more and we have the right to speak.

[*He crosses before the table rapidly and sits down beside her.*]

BERTHA

[*Turning towards him, places her left hand on his shoulder.*] Yes, Robert. I know that you like me. You need not tell me. [*Kindly.*] You need not confess any more tonight.

[*A gust of wind enters through the porch, with a sound of moving leaves. The lamp flickers quickly.*]

BERTHA

[*Pointing over his shoulder.*] Look! It is too high.

[*Without rising, he bends towards the table, and turns down the wick more. The room is half dark. The light comes in more strongly through the doorway of the bedroom.*]

ROBERT

The wind is rising. I will close that door.

BERTHA

[*Listening.*] No, it is raining still. It was only a gust of wind.

ROBERT

[*Touches her shoulder.*] Tell me if the air is too cold for you. [*Half rising.*] I will close it.

BERTHA

[*Detaining him.*] No. I am not cold. Besides, I am going now, Robert. I must.

[*Firmly.*] No, no. There is no *must* now. We were left here for this. And you are wrong, Bertha. The past is not past. It is present here now. My feeling for you is the same now as it was then, because then – you slighted it.

BERTHA

No, Robert. I did not.

ROBERT

[*Continuing.*] You did. And I have felt it all these years without knowing it – till now. Even while I lived – the kind of life you know and dislike to think of – the kind of life to which you condemned me.

BERTHA

I?

ROBERT

Yes, when you slighted the common simple gift I had to offer you – and took his gift instead.

BERTHA

[*Looking at him.*] But you never . . .

ROBERT

No. Because you had chosen him. I saw that. I saw it on the first night we met, we three together. Why did you choose him?

BERTHA

[*Bends her head.*] Is that not love?

ROBERT

[*Continuing.*] And every night when we two – he and I – came to that corner to meet you I saw it, and felt it. You remember the corner, Bertha?

BERTHA

[*As before.*] Yes.

ROBERT

And when you and he went away for your walk and I went along the street alone I felt it. And when he spoke to me about you and told me he was going away – then most of all.

BERTHA

Why then most of all?

ROBERT

Because it was then that I was guilty of my first treason
towards him.

BERTHA

Robert, what are you saying? Your first treason against Dick?

ROBERT

[Nods.] And not my last. He spoke of you and himself. Of
how your life would be together – free and all that. Free, yes!
He would not even ask you to go with him. [Bitterly.] He did
not. And you went all the same.

BERTHA

I wanted to be with him. You know . . . [Raising her head and
looking at him.] You know how we were then – Dick and I.

ROBERT

[Unheeding.] I advised him to go alone – not to take you with
him – to live alone in order to see if what he felt for you
was a passing thing which might ruin your happiness and his
career.

BERTHA

Well, Robert. It was unkind of you towards me. But I forgive
you because you were thinking of his happiness and mine.

ROBERT

[Bending closer to her.] No, Bertha. I was not. And that was
my treason. I was thinking of myself – that you might turn
from him when he had gone and he from you. Then I would
have offered you my gift. You know what it was now. The
simple common gift that men offer to women. Not the best
perhaps. Best or worse – it would have been yours.

BERTHA

[Turning away from him.] He did not take your advice.

ROBERT

[As before.] No. And the night you ran away together – O,
how happy I was!

BERTHA

[*Pressing his hands.*] Keep calm, Robert. I know you liked me always. Why did you not forget me?

ROBERT

[*Smiles bitterly.*] How happy I felt as I came back along the quays and saw in the distance the boat lit up going down the black river, taking you away from me. [*In a calmer tone.*] But why did you choose him? Did you not like me at all?

BERTHA

Yes. I liked you because you were his friend. We often spoke about you. Often and often. Every time you wrote or sent papers or books to Dick. And I like you still, Robert. [*Looking into his eyes.*] I never forgot you.

ROBERT

Nor I you. I knew I would see you again. I knew it the night you went away – that you would come back. And that was why I wrote and worked to see you again – here.

BERTHA

And here I am. You were right.

ROBERT

[*Slowly.*] Nine years. Nine times more beautiful.

BERTHA

[*Smiling.*] But am I? What do you see in me?

ROBERT

[*Gazing at her.*] A strange and beautiful lady.

BERTHA

[*Almost disgusted.*] O, please don't call me such a thing!

ROBERT

[*Earnestly.*] You are more. A young and beautiful queen.

BERTHA

[*With a sudden laugh.*] O, Robert!

ROBERT

[*Lowering his voice and bending nearer to her.*] But do you not know that you are a beautiful human being? Do you not know that you have a beautiful body? Beautiful and young?

BERTHA

[*Gravely.*] Some day I will be old.

ROBERT

[*Shakes his head.*] I cannot imagine it. Tonight you are young and beautiful. Tonight you have come back to me. [*With passion.*] Who knows what will be tomorrow? I may never see you again or never see you as I do now.

BERTHA

Would you suffer?

ROBERT

[*Looks round the room, without answering.*] This room and this hour were made for your coming. When you have gone – all is gone.

BERTHA

[*Anxiously.*] But you will see me again, Robert . . . as before.

ROBERT

[*Looks full at her.*] To make him – Richard – suffer.

BERTHA

He does not suffer.

ROBERT

[*Bowing his head.*] Yes, yes. He does.

BERTHA

He knows we like each other. Is there any harm, then?

ROBERT

[*Raising his head.*] No, there is no harm. Why should we not? He does not know yet what I feel. He has left us alone here at night, at this hour, because he longs to know it – he longs to be delivered.

BERTHA

From what?

ROBERT

[*Moves closer to her and presses her arm as he speaks.*] From every law, Bertha, from every bond. All his life he has sought to deliver himself. Every chain but one he has broken and that one we are to break, Bertha – you and I.

BERTHA

[*Almost inaudibly.*] Are you sure?

ROBERT

[*Still more warmly.*] I am sure that no law made by man is sacred before the impulse of passion. [*Almost fiercely.*] Who made us for one only? It is a crime against our own being if we are so. There is no law before impulse. Laws are for slaves. Bertha, say my name! Let me hear your voice say it. Softly!

BERTHA

[*Softly.*] Robert!

ROBERT

[*Puts his arm about her shoulder.*] Only the impulse towards youth and beauty does not die. [*He points towards the porch.*] Listen.

BERTHA

[*In alarm.*] What?

ROBERT

The rain falling. Summer rain on the earth. Night rain. The darkness and warmth and flood of passion. Tonight the earth is loved – loved and possessed. Her lover's arms around her; and she is silent. Speak, dearest!

BERTHA

[*Suddenly leans forward and listens intently.*] Hush!

ROBERT

[*Listening, smiles.*] Nothing. Nobody. We are alone.

[*A gust of wind blows in through the porch, with a sound of shaken leaves. The flame of the lamp leaps.*]

BERTHA

[*Pointing to the lamp.*] Look!

ROBERT

Only wind. We have enough light from the other room.

[*He stretches his hand across the table and puts out the lamp. The light from the doorway of the bedroom crosses the place where they sit. The room is quite dark.*]

ROBERT

Are you happy? Tell me.

BERTHA

I am going now, Robert. It is very late. Be satisfied.

ROBERT

[*Caressing her hair.*] Not yet, not yet. Tell me, do you love me a little.

BERTHA

I like you, Robert. I think you are good. [*Half rising.*] Are you satisfied?

ROBERT

[*Detaining her, kisses her hair.*] Do not go, Bertha! There is time still. Do you love me too? I have waited a long time. Do you love us both – him and also me? Do you, Bertha? The truth! Tell me. Tell me with your eyes. Or speak!

[*She does not answer. In the silence the rain is heard falling.*]

THIRD ACT

*The drawingroom of Richard Rowan's house at Merrion.
The folding doors at the right are closed and also the double
doors leading to the garden. The green plush curtains are
drawn across the window on the left. The room is half dark.
It is early in the morning of the next day. Bertha sits beside
the window, looking out between the curtains. She wears a
loose saffron dressing gown. Her hair is combed loosely over
the ears and knotted at the neck. Her hands are folded in her
lap. Her face is pale and drawn.*

> [BRIGID *comes in through the folding doors on the right
> with a featherbroom and duster. She is about to cross
> but, seeing* BERTHA, *she halts suddenly and blesses her-
> self instinctively.*]

BRIGID

Merciful hour, ma'am. You put the heart across me. Why did
you get up so early?

BERTHA

What time is it?

BRIGID

After seven, ma'am. Are you long up?

BERTHA

Some time.

BRIGID

[*Approaching her.*] Had you a bad dream that woke you?

BERTHA

I didn't sleep all night. So I got up to see the sun rise.

BRIGID

[*Opens the double doors.*] It's a lovely morning now after all
the rain we had. [*Turns round.*] But you must be dead tired,
ma'am. What will the master say at your doing a thing like

113

that? [*She goes to the door of the study and knocks.*] Master Richard!

BERTHA

[*Looks round.*] He is not there. He went out an hour ago.

BRIGID

Out there, on the strand, is it?

BERTHA

Yes.

BRIGID

[*Comes towards her and leans over the back of a chair.*] Are you fretting yourself, ma'am, about anything?

BERTHA

No, Brigid.

BRIGID

Don't be. He was always like that, meandering off by himself somewhere. He is a curious bird, Master Richard, and always was. Sure there isn't a turn in him I don't know. Are you fretting now maybe because he does be in there [*pointing to the study*] half the night at his books? Leave him alone. He'll come back to you again. Sure he thinks the sun shines out of your face, ma'am.

BERTHA

[*Sadly.*] That time is gone.

BRIGID

[*Confidentially.*] And good cause I have to remember it – that time when he was paying his addresses to you. [*She sits down beside* BERTHA: *in a lower voice.*] Do you know that he used to tell me all about you and nothing to his mother, God rest her soul? Your letters and all.

BERTHA

What? My letters to him?

BRIGID

[*Delighted.*] Yes. I can see him sitting on the kitchen table, swinging his legs and spinning out of him yards of talk about you and him and Ireland and all kinds of devilment – to an ignorant old woman like me. But that was always his way. But if he had to meet a grand highup person he'd be twice as grand himself. [*Suddenly looks at* BERTHA.] Is it crying you are now? Ah, sure, don't cry. There's good times coming still.

BERTHA

No, Brigid, that time comes only once in a lifetime. The rest of life is good for nothing except to remember that time.

BRIGID

[*Is silent for a moment: then says kindly.*] Would you like a cup of tea, ma'am? That would make you all right.

BERTHA

Yes, I would. But the milkman has not come yet.

BRIGID

No. Master Archie told me to wake him before he came. He's going out for a jaunt in the car. But I've a cup left overnight. I'll have the kettle boiling in a jiffy. Would you like a nice egg with it?

BERTHA

No, thanks.

BRIGID

Or a nice bit of toast?

BERTHA

No, Brigid, thanks. Just a cup of tea.

BRIGID

[*Crossing to the folding doors.*] I won't be a moment. [*She stops, turns back and goes towards the door on the left.*] But first I must waken Master Archie or there'll be ructions.

[*She goes out by the door on the left. After a few moments* BERTHA *rises and goes over to the study. She opens the door wide and looks in. One can see a small untidy room with many bookshelves and a large writing-table with papers and an extinguished lamp and before it*

115

a padded chair. She remains standing for some time in the doorway, then closes the door again without entering the room. She returns to her chair by the window and sits down. ARCHIE, *dressed as before, comes in by the door on the right, followed by* BRIGID.]

ARCHIE

[*Comes to her and, putting up his face to be kissed, says.*] Buon giorno, mamma!

BERTHA

[*Kissing him.*] Buon giorno, Archie! [*To* BRIGID.] Did you put another vest on him under that one?

BRIGID

He wouldn't let me, ma'am.

ARCHIE

I'm not cold, mamma.

BERTHA

I said you were to put it on, didn't I?

ARCHIE

But where is the cold?

BERTHA

[*Takes a comb from her head and combs his hair back at both sides.*] And the sleep is in your eyes still.

BRIGID

He went to bed immediately after you went out last night, ma'am.

ARCHIE

You know he's going to let me drive, mamma.

BERTHA

[*Replacing the comb in her hair, embraces him suddenly.*] O, what a big man to drive a horse!

BRIGID

Well, he's daft on horses, anyhow.

116

ARCHIE

[*Releasing himself.*] I'll make him go quick. You will see from the window, mamma. With the whip. [*He makes the gesture of cracking a whip and shouts at the top of his voice.*] Avanti!

BRIGID

Beat the poor horse, is it?

BERTHA

Come here till I clean your mouth. [*She takes her handkerchief from the pocket of her gown, wets it with her tongue and cleans his mouth.*] You're all smudges or something, dirty little creature you are.

ARCHIE

[*Repeats, laughing.*] Smudges! What is smudges?

> [*The noise is heard of a milkcan rattled on the railings before the window.*]

BRIGID

[*Draws aside the curtains and looks out.*] Here he is!

ARCHIE

[*Rapidly.*] Wait. I'm ready. Goodbye, mamma! [*He kisses her hastily and turns to go.*] Is pappie up?

BRIGID

[*Takes him by the arm.*] Come on with you now.

BERTHA

Mind yourself, Archie, and don't be **long** or I won't let you go any more.

ARCHIE

All right. Look out of the window and you'll see me. Goodbye.

> [BRIGID *and* ARCHIE *go out by the door on the left.*
> BERTHA *stands up and, drawing aside the curtains still more, stands in the embrasure of the window looking out. The hall door is heard opening: then a slight noise of voices and cans is heard. The door is closed. After a moment or two* BERTHA *is seen waving her hand gaily in a salute.* BRIGID *enters and stands behind her, looking over her shoulder.*]

BRIGID

Look at the sit of him! As serious as you like.

BERTHA

[*Suddenly withdrawing from her post.*] Stand out of the window. I don't want to be seen.

BRIGID

Why, ma'am, what is it?

BERTHA

[*Crossing towards the folding doors.*] Say I'm not up, that I'm not well. I can't see anyone.

BRIGID

[*Follows her.*] Who is it, ma'am?

BERTHA

[*Halting.*] Wait a moment.

[*She listens. A knock is heard at the hall door.*]

BERTHA

[*Stands a moment in doubt, then.*] No, say I'm in.

BRIGID

[*In doubt.*] Here!

BERTHA

[*Hurriedly.*] Yes. Say I have just got up.

[BRIGID *goes out on the left.* BERTHA *goes towards the double doors and fingers the curtains nervously, as if settling them. The hall door is heard to open. Then* BEATRICE JUSTICE *enters and, as* BERTHA *does not turn at once, stands in hesitation near the door on the left. She is dressed as before and has a newspaper in her hand.*]

BEATRICE

[*Advances rapidly.*] Mrs Rowan, excuse me for coming at such an hour.

BERTHA

[*Turns.*] Good morning, Miss Justice. [*She comes towards her.*] Is anything the matter?

BEATRICE

[*Nervously.*] I don't know. That is what I wanted to ask you.

BERTHA

[*Looks curiously at her.*] You are out of breath. Won't you sit down?

BEATRICE

[*Sitting down.*] Thank you.

BERTHA

[*Sits opposite her, pointing to her paper.*] Is there something in the paper?

BEATRICE

[*Laughs nervously: opens the paper.*] Yes.

BERTHA

About Dick?

BEATRICE

Yes. Here it is. A long article, a leading article, by my cousin. All his life is here. Do you wish to see it?

BERTHA

[*Takes the paper, and opens it.*] Where is it?

BEATRICE

In the middle. It is headed: A *Distinguished Irishman.*

BERTHA

Is it . . . for Dick or against him?

BEATRICE

[*Warmly.*] O, for him! You can read what he says about Mr Rowan. And I know that Robert stayed in town very late last night to write it.

BERTHA

[*Nervously.*] Yes. Are you sure?

BEATRICE

Yes. Very late. I heard him come home. It was long after two.

BERTHA

[*Watching her.*] It alarmed you? I mean to be awakened at that hour of the morning.

BEATRICE

I am a light sleeper. But I knew he had come from the office and then ... I suspected he had written an article about Mr Rowan and that was why he came so late.

BERTHA

How quick you were to think of that?

BEATRICE

Well, after what took place here yesterday afternoon – I mean what Robert said, that Mr Rowan had accepted this position. It was only natural I should think ...

BERTHA

Ah, yes. Naturally.

BEATRICE

[*Hastily.*] But that is not what alarmed me. But immediately after I heard a noise in my cousin's room.

BERTHA

[*Crumples together the paper in her hands, breathlessly.*] My God! What is it? Tell me.

BEATRICE

[*Observing her.*] Why does that upset you so much?

BERTHA

[*Sinking back, with a forced laugh.*] Yes, of course, it is very foolish of me. My nerves are all upset. I slept very badly, too. That is why I got up so early. But tell me what was it then?

BEATRICE

Only the noise of his valise being pulled along the floor. Then I heard him walking about his room, whistling softly. And then locking it and strapping it.

BERTHA

He is going away!

BEATRICE

That was what alarmed me. I feared he had had a quarrel with Mr Rowan and that his article was an attack.

BERTHA

But why should they quarrel? Have you noticed anything between them?

BEATRICE

I thought I did. A coldness.

BERTHA

Lately?

BEATRICE

For some time past.

BERTHA

[Smoothing the paper out.] Do you know the reason?

BEATRICE

[Hesitatingly.] No.

BERTHA

[After a pause.] Well, but if this article is for him, as you say, they have not quarrelled. [She reflects a moment.] And written last night, too.

BEATRICE

Yes. I bought the paper at once to see. But why, then, is he going away so suddenly? I feel that there is something wrong. I feel that something has happened between them.

BERTHA

Would you be sorry?

BEATRICE

I would be very sorry. You see, Mrs Rowan, Robert is my first cousin and it would grieve me very deeply, if he were to treat Mr Rowan badly, now that he has come back, or if they had a serious quarrel especially because . . .

BERTHA

[Toying with the paper.] Because?

121

BEATRICE

Because it was my cousin who urged Mr Rowan always to come back. I have that on my conscience.

BERTHA

It should be on Mr Hand's conscience, should it not?

BEATRICE

[*Uncertainly.*] On mine, too. Because – I spoke to my cousin about Mr Rowan when he was away and, to a certain extent, it was I . . .

BERTHA

[*Nods slowly.*] I see. And that is on your conscience. Only that?

BEATRICE

I think so.

BERTHA

[*Almost cheerfully.*] It looks as if it was you, Miss Justice, who brought my husband back to Ireland.

BEATRICE

I, Mrs Rowan?

BERTHA

Yes, you. By your letters to him and then by speaking to your cousin as you said just now. Do you not think that you are the person who brought him back?

BEATRICE

[*Blushing suddenly.*] No. I could not think that.

BERTHA

[*Watches her for a moment; then turning aside.*] You know that my husband is writing very much since he came back.

BEATRICE

Is he?

BERTHA

Did you not know? [*She points towards the study.*] He passes the great part of the night in there writing. Night after night.

BEATRICE

In his study?

BERTHA

Study or bedroom. You may call it what you please. He sleeps there, too, on a sofa. He slept there last night. I can show you if you don't believe me.

[She rises to go towards the study. BEATRICE half rises quickly and makes a gesture of refusal.]

BEATRICE

I believe you, of course, Mrs Rowan, when you tell me.

BERTHA

[Sitting down again.] Yes. He is writing. And it must be about something which has come into his life lately – since we came back to Ireland. Some change. Do you know that any change has come into his life? [She looks searchingly at her.] Do you know it or feel it?

BEATRICE

[Answers her look steadily.] Mrs Rowan, that is not a question to ask me. If any change has come into his life since he came back you must know and feel it.

BERTHA

You could know it just as well. You are very intimate in this house.

BEATRICE

I am not the only person who is intimate here.

[They both look at each other coldly in silence for some moments. BERTHA lays aside the paper and sits down on a chair nearer to BEATRICE.]

BERTHA

[Placing her hand on BEATRICE's knee.] So you also hate me, Miss Justice?

BEATRICE

[With an effort.] Hate you? I?

123

BERTHA

[*Insistently but softly.*] Yes. You know what it means to hate a person?

BEATRICE

Why should I hate you? I have never hated anyone.

BERTHA

Have you ever loved anyone? [*She puts her hand on* BEAT-RICE's *wrist.*] Tell me. You have?

BEATRICE

[*Also softly.*] Yes. In the past.

BERTHA

Not now?

BEATRICE

No.

BERTHA

Can you say that to me – truly. Look at me.

BEATRICE

[*Looks at her.*] Yes, I can.

[*A short pause.* BERTHA *withdraws her hand, and turns away her head in some embarrassment.*]

BERTHA

You said just now that another person is intimate in this house. You meant your cousin . . . Was it he?

BEATRICE

Yes.

BERTHA

Have you not forgotten him?

BEATRICE

[*Quietly.*] I have tried to.

BERTHA

[*Clasping her hands.*] You hate me. You think I am happy. If you only knew how wrong you are!

BEATRICE

[*Shakes her head.*] I do not.

BERTHA

Happy! When I do not understand anything that he writes, when I cannot help him in any way, when I don't even understand half of what he says to me sometimes! You could and you can. [*Excitedly.*] But I am afraid for him, afraid for both of them. [*She stands up suddenly and goes towards the davenport.*] He must not go away like that. [*She takes a writing pad from the drawer and writes a few lines in great haste.*] No, it is impossible! Is he mad to do such a thing? [*Turning to* BEATRICE.] Is he still at home?

BEATRICE

[*Watching her in wonder.*] Yes. Have you written to him to ask him to come here?

BERTHA

[*Rises.*] I have. I will send Brigid across with it. Brigid!

[*She goes out by the door on the left rapidly.*]

BEATRICE

[*Gazing after her, instinctively.*] It is true, then!

[*She glances towards the door of* RICHARD's *study and catches her head in her hands. Then, recovering herself, she takes the paper from the little table, opens it, takes a spectacle case from her handbag and, putting on a pair of spectacles, bends down, reading it.* RICHARD ROWAN *enters from the garden. He is dressed as before but wears a soft hat and carries a thin cane.*]

RICHARD

[*Stands in the doorway, observing her for some moments.*] There are demons [*he points towards the strand*] out there. I heard them jabbering since dawn.

BEATRICE

[*Starts to her feet.*] Mr Rowan!

RICHARD

I assure you. The isle is full of voices. Yours also, *Otherwise*

I could not see you, it said. And her voice. But, I assure you, they are all demons. I made the sign of the cross upside down and that silenced them.

BEATRICE

[*Stammering.*] I came here, Mr Rowan, so early because . . . to show you this . . . Robert wrote it . . . about you . . . last night.

RICHARD

[*Takes off his hat.*] My dear Miss Justice, you told me yesterday, I think, why you came here and I never forget anything. [*Advancing towards her, holding out his hand.*] Good morning.

BEATRICE

[*Suddenly takes off her spectacles and places the paper in his hands.*] I came for this. It is an article about you. Robert wrote it last night. Will you read it?

RICHARD

[*Bows.*] Read it now? Certainly.

BEATRICE

[*Looks at him in despair.*] O, Mr Rowan, it makes me suffer to look at you.

RICHARD

[*Opens and reads the paper.*] Death of the Very Reverend Canon Mulhall. Is that it?

> [BERTHA *appears at the door on the left and stands to listen.*]

RICHARD

[*Turns over a page.*] Yes, here we are! A *Distinguished Irishman.* [*He begins to read in a rather loud hard voice.*] Not the least vital of the problems which confront our country is the problem of her attitude towards those of her children who, having left her in her hour of need, have been called back to her now on the eve of her longawaited victory, to her whom in loneliness and exile they have at last learned to love. In exile, we have said, but here we must distinguish. There is an economic and there is a spiritual exile. There are those who left her to seek the bread by which men live and there are others, nay, her most favoured children, who left her to seek in other lands that food of the spirit by which a nation of human beings is sustained in life. Those who recall the intellectual life of Dublin of a decade since will have many memories of Mr Rowan. Something of that fierce indignation which lacerated the heart . . .

[*He raises his eyes from the paper and sees* BERTHA *standing in the doorway. Then he lays aside the paper and looks at her. A long silence.*]

BEATRICE

[*With an effort.*] You see, Mr Rowan, your day has dawned at last. Even here. And you see that you have a warm friend in Robert, a friend who understands you.

RICHARD

Did you notice the little phrase at the beginning: *those who left her in her hour of need?*

[*He looks searchingly at* BERTHA, *turns and walks into his study, closing the door behind him.*]

BERTHA

[*Speaking half to herself.*] I gave up everything for him, religion, family, my own peace.

[*She sits down heavily in an armchair.* BEATRICE *comes towards her.*]

BEATRICE

[*Weakly.*] But do you not feel also that Mr Rowan's ideas . . .

BERTHA

[*Bitterly.*] Ideas and ideas! But the people in this world have other ideas or pretend to. They have to put up with him in spite of his ideas because he is able to do something. Me, no. I am nothing.

BEATRICE

You stand by his side.

BERTHA

[*With increasing bitterness.*] Ah, nonsense, Miss Justice! I am

127

only a thing he got entangled with and my son is – the nice name they give those children. Do you think I am a stone? Do you think I don't see it in their eyes and in their manner when they have to meet me?

BEATRICE

Do not let them humble you, Mrs Rowan.

BERTHA

[*Haughtily.*] Humble me! I am very proud of myself, if you want to know. What have they ever done for him? I made him a man. What are they all in his life? No more than the dirt under his boots! [*She stands up and walks excitedly to and fro.*] He can despise me, too, like the rest of them – now. And you can despise me. But you will never humble me, any of you.

BEATRICE

Why do you accuse me?

BERTHA

[*Going to her impulsively.*] I am in such suffering. Excuse me if I was rude. I want us to be friends. [*She holds out her hands.*] Will you?

BEATRICE

[*Taking her hands.*] Gladly.

BERTHA

[*Looking at her.*] What lovely long eyelashes you have! And your eyes have such a sad expression!

BEATRICE

[*Smilingly.*] I see very little with them. They are very weak.

BERTHA

[*Warmly.*] But beautiful.

[*She embraces her quietly and kisses her. Then withdraws from her a little shyly.* BRIGID *comes in from the left.*]

BRIGID

I gave it to himself, ma'am.

128

Did he send a message?

BRIGID

He was just going out, ma'am. He told me to say he'd be here after me.

BERTHA

Thanks.

BRIGID

[*Going.*] Would you like the tea and the toast now, ma'am?

BERTHA

Not now, Brigid. After perhaps. When Mr Hand comes show him in at once.

BRIGID

Yes, ma'am.

[*She goes out on the left.*]

BEATRICE

I will go now, Mrs Rowan, before he comes.

BERTHA

[*Somewhat timidly.*] Then we are friends?

BEATRICE

[*In the same tone.*] We will try to be. [*Turning.*] Do you allow me to go out through the garden? I don't want to meet my cousin now.

BERTHA

Of course. [*She takes her hand.*] It is so strange that we spoke like this now. But I always wanted to. Did you?

BEATRICE

I think I did, too.

BERTHA

[*Smiling.*] Even in Rome. When I went out for a walk with Archie I used to think about you, what you were like, because I knew about you from Dick. I used to look at different persons, coming out of churches or going by in carriages, and think that perhaps they were like you. Because Dick told me you were dark.

BEATRICE

[*Again nervously.*] Really?

BERTHA

[*Pressing her hand.*] Goodbye then – for the present.

BEATRICE

[*Disengaging her hand.*] Good morning.

BERTHA

I will see you to the gate.

[*She accompanies her out through the double doors. They go down through the garden.* RICHARD ROWAN *comes in from the study. He halts near the doors, looking down the garden. Then he turns away, comes to the little table, takes up the paper and reads.* BERTHA, *after some moments, appears in the doorway and stands watching him till he has finished. He lays down the paper again and turns to go back to his study.*]

BERTHA

Dick!

RICHARD

[*Stopping.*] Well?

BERTHA

You have not spoken to me.

RICHARD

I have nothing to say. Have you?

BERTHA

Do you not wish to know – about what happened last night?

RICHARD

That I will never know.

BERTHA

I will tell you if you ask me.

RICHARD

You will tell me. But I will never know. Never in this world.

BERTHA

[*Moving towards him.*] I will tell you the truth, Dick, as I always told you. I never lied to you.

RICHARD

[*Clenching his hands in the air, passionately.*] Yes, yes. The truth! But I will never know, I tell you.

BERTHA

Why, then, did you leave me last night?

RICHARD

[*Bitterly.*] In your hour of need.

BERTHA

[*Threateningly.*] You urged me to it. Not because you love me. If you loved me or if you knew what love was you would not have left me. For your own sake you urged me to it.

RICHARD

I did not make myself. I am what I am.

BERTHA

To have it always to throw against me. To make me humble before you, as you always did. To be free yourself. [*Pointing towards the garden.*] With her! And that is your love! Every word you say is false.

RICHARD

[*Controlling himself.*] It is useless to ask you to listen to me.

BERTHA

Listen to you! She is the person for listening. Why would you waste your time with me? Talk to her.

RICHARD

[*Nods his head.*] I see. You have driven her away from me now, as you drove everyone else from my side – every friend I ever had, every human being that ever tried to approach me. You hate her.

[*Warmly.*] No such thing! I think you have made her unhappy as you have made me and as you made your dead
mother unhappy and killed her. Womankiller! That is your
name.

RICHARD

[*Turns to go.*] Arrivederci!

BERTHA

[*Excitedly.*] She is a fine and high character. I like her. She is
everything that I am not – in birth and education. You tried
to ruin her but you could not. Because she is well able for you
– what I am not. And you know it.

RICHARD

[*Almost shouting.*] What the devil are you talking about her
for?

BERTHA

[*Clasping her hands.*] O, how I wish I had never met you!
How I curse that day!

RICHARD

[*Bitterly.*] I am in the way, is it? You would like to be free
now. You have only to say the word.

BERTHA

[*Proudly.*] Whenever you like I am ready.

RICHARD

So that you could meet your lover – freely?

BERTHA

Yes.

RICHARD

Night after night?

BERTHA

[*Gazing before her and speaking with intense passion.*] To
meet my lover! [*Holding out her arms before her.*] My lover!
Yes! My lover!

[*She bursts suddenly into tears and sinks down on a chair, covering her face with her hands.* RICHARD *approaches her slowly and touches her on the shoulder.*]

RICHARD

Bertha! [*She does not answer.*] Bertha, you are free.

BERTHA

[*Pushes his hand aside and starts to her feet.*] Don't touch me! You are a stranger to me. You do not understand anything in me – not one thing in my heart or soul. A stranger! I am living with a stranger!

[*A knock is heard at the hall door.* BERTHA *dries her eyes quickly with her handkerchief and settles the front of her gown.* RICHARD *listens for a moment, looks at her keenly and, turning away, walks into his study.* ROBERT HAND *enters from the left. He is dressed in dark brown and carries in his hand a brown Alpine hat.*]

ROBERT

[*Closing the door quietly behind him.*] You sent for me.

BERTHA

[*Rises.*] Yes. Are you mad to think of going away like that – without even coming here – without saying anything?

ROBERT

[*Advancing towards the table on which the paper lies, glances at it.*] What I have to say I said here.

BERTHA

When did you write it? Last night – after I went away?

ROBERT

[*Gracefully.*] To be quite accurate I wrote part of it – in my mind – before you went away. The rest – the worst part – I wrote after. Much later.

BERTHA

And you could write last night!

ROBERT

[*Shrugs his shoulders.*] I am a welltrained animal. [*He comes closer to her.*] I passed a long wandering night after . . . in my office, at the vicechancellor's house, in a nightclub, in the streets, in my room. Your image was always before my eyes, your hand in my hand, Bertha, I will never forget last night. [*He lays his hat on the table and takes her hand.*] Why do you not look at me? May I not touch you?

BERTHA

[*Points to the study.*] Dick is in there.

ROBERT

[*Drops her hand.*] In that case children be good.

BERTHA

Where are you going?

ROBERT

To foreign parts. That is, to my cousin Jack Justice, *alias* Doggy Justice, in Surrey. He has a nice country place there and the air is mild.

BERTHA

Why are you going?

ROBERT

[*Looks at her in silence.*] Can you not guess one reason?

BERTHA

On account of me?

ROBERT

Yes. It is not pleasant for me to remain here just now.

BERTHA

[*Sits down helplessly.*] But this is cruel of you, Robert. Cruel to me and to him also.

ROBERT

Has he asked . . . what happened?

BERTHA

[*Joining her hands in despair.*] No. He refuses to ask me anything. He says he will never know.

134

ROBERT

[*Nods gravely.*] Richard is right there. He is always right.

BERTHA

But, Robert, you must speak to him.

ROBERT

What am I to say to him?

BERTHA

The truth! Everything!

ROBERT

[*Reflects.*] No, Bertha. I am a man speaking to a man. I cannot tell him everything.

BERTHA

He will believe that you are going away because you are afraid to face him after last night.

ROBERT

[*After a pause.*] Well, I am not a coward any more than he. I will see him.

BERTHA

[*Rises.*] I will call him.

ROBERT

[*Catching her hands.*] Bertha! What happened last night? What is the truth that I am to tell? [*He gazes earnestly into her eyes.*] Were you mine in that sacred night of love? Or have I dreamed it?

BERTHA

[*Smiles faintly.*] Remember your dream of me. You dreamed that I was yours last night.

ROBERT

And that is the truth – a dream? That is what I am to tell?

BERTHA

Yes.

ROBERT

[*Kisses both her hands.*] Bertha! [*In a softer voice.*] In all my life only that dream is real. I forget the rest. [*He kisses her hands again.*] And now I can tell him the truth. Call him.

[BERTHA *goes to the door of* RICHARD's *study and knocks. There is no answer. She knocks again.*]

BERTHA

Dick! [*There is no answer.*] Mr Hand is here. He wants to speak to you, to say goodbye. He is going away. [*There is no answer. She beats her hand loudly on the panel of the door and calls in an alarmed voice.*] Dick! Answer me!

[RICHARD ROWAN *comes in from the study. He comes at once to* ROBERT *but does not hold out his hand.*]

RICHARD

[*Calmly.*] I thank you for your kind article about me. Is it true that you have come to say goodbye?

ROBERT

There is nothing to thank me for, Richard. Now and always I am your friend. Now more than ever before. Do you believe me, Richard?

[RICHARD *sits down on a chair and buries his face in his hands.* BERTHA *and* ROBERT *gaze at each other in silence. Then she turns away and goes out quietly on the right.* ROBERT *goes towards* RICHARD *and stands near him, resting his hands on the back of a chair, looking down at him. There is a long silence. A* FISHWOMAN *is heard crying out as she passes along the road outside.*]

THE FISHWOMAN

Fresh Dublin bay herrings! Fresh Dublin bay herrings! Dublin bay herrings!

ROBERT

[*Quietly.*] I will tell you the truth, Richard. Are you listening?

RICHARD

[*Raises his face and leans back to listen.*] Yes.

[ROBERT *sits on the chair beside him. The* FISHWOMAN *is heard calling out farther away.*]

THE FISHWOMAN

Fresh herrings! Dublin bay herrings!

ROBERT

I failed, Richard. That is the truth. Do you believe me?

RICHARD

I am listening.

ROBERT

I failed. She is yours, as she was nine years ago, when you met her first.

RICHARD

When we met her first, you mean.

ROBERT

Yes. [*He looks down for some moments.*] Shall I go on?

RICHARD

Yes.

ROBERT

She went away. I was left alone – for the second time. I went to the vicechancellor's house and dined. I said you were ill and would come another night. I made epigrams new and old – that one about the statues also. I drank claret cup. I went to my office and wrote my article. Then ...

RICHARD

Then?

ROBERT

Then I went to a certain nightclub. There were men there – and also women. At least, they looked like women. I danced with one of them. She asked me to see her home. Shall I go on?

RICHARD

Yes.

ROBERT

I saw her home in a cab. She lives near Donnybrook. In the cab took place what the subtle Duns Scotus calls a death of the spirit. Shall I go on?

RICHARD

Yes.

ROBERT

She wept. She told me she was the divorced wife of a barrister. I offered her a sovereign as she told me she was short of money. She would not take it and wept very much. Then she drank some melissa water from a little bottle which she had in her satchel. I saw her enter her house. Then I walked home. In my room I found that my coat was all stained with the melissa water. I had no luck even with my coats yesterday: that was the second one. The idea came to me then to change my suit and go away by the morning boat. I packed my valise and went to bed. I am going away by the next train to my cousin, Jack Justice, in Surrey. Perhaps for a fortnight. Perhaps longer. Are you disgusted?

RICHARD

Why did you not go by the boat?

ROBERT

I slept it out.

RICHARD

You intended to go without saying goodbye – without coming here?

ROBERT

Yes.

RICHARD

Why?

ROBERT

My story is not very nice, is it?

RICHARD

But you have come.

ROBERT

Bertha sent me a message to come.

RICHARD

But for that . . .?

ROBERT

But for that I should not have come.

RICHARD

Did it strike you that if you had gone without coming here I should have understood it – in my own way?

ROBERT

Yes, it did.

RICHARD

What, then, do you wish me to believe?

ROBERT

I wish you to believe that I failed. That Bertha is yours now as she was nine years ago, when you – when we – met her first.

RICHARD

Do you want to know what I did?

ROBERT

No.

RICHARD

I came home at once.

ROBERT

Did you hear Bertha return?

RICHARD

No. I wrote all the night. And thought. [*Pointing to the study.*] In there. Before dawn I went out and walked the strand from end to end.

ROBERT

[*Shaking his head.*] Suffering. Torturing yourself.

RICHARD

Hearing voices about me. The voices of those who say they love me.

ROBERT

[*Points to the door on the right.*] One. And mine?

RICHARD

Another still.

ROBERT

[*Smiles and touches his forehead with his right forefinger.*] True. My interesting but somewhat melancholy cousin. And what did they tell you?

RICHARD

They told me to despair.

ROBERT

A queer way of showing their love, I must say! And will you despair?

RICHARD

[*Rising.*] No.

[*A noise is heard at the window.* ARCHIE's *face is seen flattened against one of the panes. He is heard calling.*]

ARCHIE

Open the window! Open the window!

ROBERT

[*Looks at* RICHARD.] Did you hear his voice, too, Richard, with the others — out there on the strand? Your son's voice. [*Smiling.*] Listen! How full it is of despair!

ARCHIE

Open the window, please, will you?

ROBERT

Perhaps, there, Richard, is the freedom we seek — you in one way, I in another. In him and not in us. Perhaps . . .

Perhaps . . .?

ROBERT

I said *perhaps*. I would say almost surely if . . .

RICHARD

If what?

ROBERT

[*With a faint smile.*] If he were mine.

[*He goes to the window and opens it.* ARCHIE *scrambles in.*]

ROBERT

Like yesterday – eh?

ARCHIE

Good morning, Mr Hand. [*He runs to* RICHARD *and kisses him.*] *Buon giorno, babbo.*

RICHARD

Buon giorno, Archie.

ROBERT

And where were you, my young gentleman?

ARCHIE

Out with the milkman. I drove the horse. We went to Booterstown. [*He takes off his cap and throws it on a chair.*] I am very hungry.

ROBERT

[*Takes his hat from the table.*] Richard, goodbye. [*Offering his hand.*] To our next meeting!

RICHARD

[*Rises, touches his hand.*] Goodbye.

[BERTHA *appears at the door on the right.*]

ROBERT

[*Catches sight of her: to* ARCHIE.] Get your cap. Come on with me. I'll buy you a cake and I'll tell you a story.

ARCHIE

[*To* BERTHA.] May I, mamma?

BERTHA

Yes.

ARCHIE

[*Takes his cap.*] I am ready.

ROBERT

[*To* RICHARD *and* BERTHA.] Goodbye to pappa and mamma.
But not a big goodbye.

ARCHIE

Will you tell me a fairy story, Mr Hand?

ROBERT

A fairy story? Why not? I am your fairy godfather.

[*They go out together through the double doors and
down the garden. When they have gone* BERTHA *goes to*
RICHARD *and puts her arm round his waist.*]

BERTHA

Dick, dear, do you believe now that I have been true to you?
Last night and always.

RICHARD

[*Sadly.*] Do not ask me, Bertha.

BERTHA

[*Pressing him more closely.*] I have been, dear. Surely you
believe me. I gave you myself – all. I gave up all for you. You
took me – and you left me.

RICHARD

When did I leave you?

BERTHA

You left me: and I waited for you to come back to me. Dick
dear, come here to me. Sit down. How tired you must be!

[*She draws him towards the lounge. He sits down,
almost reclining, resting on his arm. She sits on the mat
before the lounge, holding his hand.*]

142

BERTHA

Yes, dear. I waited for you. Heavens, what I suffered then – when we lived in Rome! Do you remember the terrace of our house?

RICHARD

Yes.

BERTHA

I used to sit there, waiting, with the poor child with his toys, waiting till he got sleepy. I could see all the roofs of the city and the river, the *Tevere*. What is its name?

RICHARD

The Tiber.

BERTHA

[*Caressing her cheek with his hand.*] It was lovely, Dick, only I was so sad. I was alone, Dick, forgotten by you and by all. I felt my life was ended.

RICHARD

It had not begun.

BERTHA

And I used to look at the sky, so beautiful, without a cloud and the city you said was so old: and then I used to think of Ireland and about ourselves.

RICHARD

Ourselves?

BERTHA

Yes. Ourselves. Not a day passes that I do not see ourselves, you and me, as we were when we met first. Every day of my life I see that. Was I not true to you all that time?

RICHARD

[*Sighs deeply.*] Yes, Bertha. You were my bride in exile.

BERTHA

Wherever you go, I will follow you. If you wish to go away now I will go with you.

RICHARD

I will remain. It is too soon yet to despair.

BERTHA

[*Again caressing his hand.*] It is not true that I want to drive everyone from you. I wanted to bring you close together – you and him. Speak to me. Speak out all your heart to me. What you feel and what you suffer.

RICHARD

I am wounded, Bertha.

BERTHA

How wounded, dear? Explain to me what you mean. I will try to understand everything you say. In what way are you wounded?

RICHARD

[*Releases his hand and, taking her head between his hands, bends it back and gazes long into her eyes.*] I have a deep, deep wound of doubt in my soul.

BERTHA

[*Motionless.*] Doubt of me?

RICHARD

Yes.

BERTHA

I am yours. [*In a whisper.*] If I died this moment, I am yours.

RICHARD

[*Still gazing at her and speaking as if to an absent person.*] I have wounded my soul for you – a deep wound of doubt which can never be healed. I can never know, never in this world. I do not wish to know or to believe. I do not care. It is not in the darkness of belief that I desire you. But in restless living wounding doubt. To hold you by no bonds, even of love, to be united with you in body and soul in utter nakedness – for this I longed. And now I am tired for a while, Bertha. My wound tires me.

[*He stretches himself out wearily along the lounge.* BERTHA *holds his hand, still speaking very softly.*]

Forget me, Dick. Forget me and love me again as you did the first time. I want my lover. To meet him, to go to him, to give myself to him. You, Dick. O, my strange wild lover, come back to me again!

[*She closes her eyes.*]

Notes by the Author

RICHARD – an automystic
ROBERT – an automobile.

The soul like the body may have a virginity. For the woman to yield it or for the man to take it is the act of love. Love (understood as the desire of good for another) is in fact so unnatural a phenomenon that it can scarcely repeat itself, the soul being unable to become virgin again and not having energy enough to cast itself out again into the ocean of another's soul. It is the repressed consciousness of this inability and lack of spiritual energy which explains Bertha's mental paralysis.

Her age: 28. Robert likens her to the moon because of her dress. Her age is the completion of a lunar rhythm. Cf. Oriani on menstrual flow – *la malattia sacra che in un rituo lunare prepara la donna per il sacrificio.*

Robert wishes Richard to use against him the weapons which social conventions and morals put in the hands of the husband. Richard refuses. Bertha wishes Richard to use these weapons also in her defence. Richard refuses also and for the same reason. His defence of her soul and body is an invisible and imponderable sword. As a contribution to the study of jealousy Shakespeare's *Othello* is incomplete. It and Spinoza's analysis are made from the sensationalist standpoint – Spinoza speaks of *pudendis et excrementis alterius jungere imaginem rei amatae.* Bertha has considered the passion in itself – apart from hatred or baffled lust, the scholastic definition of jealousy as a *passio irascibilis* comes nearer – its object being a difficult good. In this play Richard's jealousy is carried one step nearer to its own heart. Separated from hatred and having its baffled lust converted into an erotic stimulus and moreover holding in its own power the hindrance, the difficulty which has excited it, it must reveal itself

147

as the very immolation of the pleasure of possession on the altar of love. He is jealous, wills and knows his own dishonour and the dishonour of her, to be united with every phase of whose being is love's end, as to achieve that union in the region of the difficult, the void and the impossible is its necessary tendency.

It will be difficult to recommend Beatrice to the interest of the audience, every man of which is Robert and would like to be Richard – in any case Bertha's. The note of compassion can be struck when she takes the spectacles from her pocket in order to read. Critics may say what they like, all these persons – even Bertha – are suffering during the action.

Why the title *Exiles*? A nation exacts a penance from those who dared to leave her payable on their return. The elder brother in the fable of the Prodigal Son is Robert Hand. The father took the side of the prodigal. This is probably not the way of the world – certainly not in Ireland: but Jesus' Kingdom was not of this world nor was or is his wisdom.

Bertha's state when abandoned spiritually by Richard must be expressed by the actress by a suggestion of hypnosis. Her state is like that of Jesus in the garden of olives. It is the soul of woman left naked and alone that it may come to an understanding of its own nature. She must appear also to be carried forward to the last point consistent with her immunity by the current of the action and must show even a point of resentment against the man who will not hold out a hand to save her. Through these experiences she will suffuse her own reborn temperament with the wonder of her soul at its own solitude and at her beauty, formed and dissolving itself eternally amid the clouds of mortality.

The secondary and lower phase of Robert's position is the suspicion that Richard is a cunning adventurer using Bertha's body as a bait to gain Robert's friendship and support. The corresponding phase in Richard's attitude is the suspicion that Robert's admiration and friendship for him is simulated in order to lull and stupefy the vigilance of his mind. Both these suspicions are borne in upon the characters from purely external evidence and do not in either case spring into existence spontaneously from the soils of their natures.

It is an irony of the play that while Robert not Richard is the apostle of beauty, beauty in its visible and invisible being is present under Richard's roof.

Since the publication of the lost pages of *Madame Bovary* the centre of sympathy appears to have been esthetically shifted from the lover or fancyman to the husband or cuckold. This displacement is also rendered more stable by the gradual growth of a collective practical realism due to changed economic conditions in the mass of the people who are called to hear and feel a work of art relating to their lives. This change is utilized in *Exiles* although the union of Richard and Bertha is irregular to the extent that the spiritual revolt of Richard which would be strange and ill-welcomed otherwise can enter into combat with Robert's decrepit prudence with some chance of fighting before the public a drawn battle. Praga in *La Crisi* and Giacosa in *Tristi Amori* have understood and profited by this change but have not used it, as is done here, as a technical shield for the protection of a delicate, strange, and highly sensitive conscience.

Robert is convinced of the non-existence, of the unreality of the spiritual facts which exist and are real for Richard, the action of the piece should however convince Robert of the existence and reality of Richard's mystical defence of his wife. If this defence be a reality how can those facts on which it is based be then unreal?

It would be interesting to make some sketches of Bertha if she had united her life for nine years to Robert – not necessarily in the way of drama but rather impressionist sketches. For instance, Mrs Robert Hand (because he intended to do it decently) ordering carpets in Grafton Street, at Leopardstown races, provided with a seat on the platform at the unveiling of a statue, putting out the lights in the drawing room after a social evening in her husband's house, kneeling outside a confessional in the jesuit church.

Richard has fallen from a higher world and is indignant when he discovers baseness in men and women. Robert has risen from a lower world and so far is he from indignation that it surprises him that men and women are not baser and more ignoble.

ROBERT, *nods:* Yes, you won. I saw your triumph.

RICHARD, *rising suddenly:* Excuse me, I forgot. Will you have some whisky?

ROBERT: All things come to those who wait.

RICHARD *goes to the sideboard and fills out a glass of whisky from the decanter and brings it with a small carafe of water to the table.*

RICHARD, *lolling back on the couch:* Will you add the water yourself?

ROBERT, *does so:* And you?

RICHARD, *shaking his head:* Nothing.

ROBERT, *holding his glass:* I think of our wild nights long ago, our nights of revelry and talk and carousing.

RICHARD: In our house.

ROBERT, *raising his glass:* Prosit!

When Richard left the church he met many men of the same type as Robert.

Problem: Archie, Richard's son, is brought up on Robert's principles.

Beatrice has had an interview with her mother before she enters in the first act.

Bertha alludes to Beatrice as her ladyship.

N.(B.) – 12 Nov. 1913
   Garter: precious, Prezioso, Bodkin, music, palegreen, brace-
      let, cream sweets, lily of the valley, convent garden
      (Galway), sea.

Rat: Sickness, disgust, poverty, cheese, woman's ear, (child's ear?)

Dagger: heart, death, soldier, war, band, judgment, king.

N.(B.) – 13 Nov. 1913

Moon: Shelley's grave in Rome. He is rising from it: blond she weeps for him. He has fought in vain for an ideal and died killed by the world. Yet he rises. Graveyard at Rahoon by moonlight where Bodkin's grave is. He lies in the grave. She sees his tomb (family vault) and weeps. The name is homely. Shelley's is strange and wild. He is dark, unrisen, killed by love and life, young. The earth holds him.

Bodkin died. Kearns died. In the convent they called her the man-killer: (woman-killer was one of her names for me). I live in soul and body.

She is the earth, dark, formless, mother, made beautiful by the moonlit night, darkly conscious of her instincts. Shelley whom she has held in her womb or grave rises: the part of Richard which neither love nor life can do away with; the part for which she loves him: the part she must try to kill, never be able to kill and rejoice at her impotence. Her tears are of worship, Magdalen seeing the arisen Lord in the garden where he had been laid in the tomb. Rome is the strange world and strange life to which Richard brings her. Rahoon her people. She weeps over Rahoon too, over him whom her love has killed, the dark boy whom, as the earth, she embraces in death and disintegration. He is her buried life, her past. His attendant images are the trinkets and toys of girl-hood (bracelet, cream sweets, palegreen lily of the valley, the convent garden). His symbols are music and the sea, liquid formless earth, in which are buried the drowned soul and body. There are tears of commiseration. She is Magdalen who weeps remembering the loves she could not return.

If Robert really prepares the way for Richard's advance and hopes for it while he tries at the same time secretly to combat this advance by destroying at a blow Richard's confidence in himself the position is like that of Wotan who in willing the birth and growth of Siegfried longs for his own destruction. Every step advanced by humanity through Richard is a step backwards by the type which Robert stands for.

Richard fears the reaction inevitable in Robert's temperament: and not for Bertha's sake only, that is, not to feel that he by standing aside has allowed her to go her way through a passing love to neglect but to feel that a woman chosen by him has been set aside for another not chosen by him.

Beatrice's mind is an abandoned cold temple in which hymns have risen heavenward in a distant past but where now a doddering priest offers alone and hopelessly prayers to the Most High.

Richard having first understood the nature of innocence when it has been lost by him fears to believe that Bertha, to understand the chastity of her nature, must first lose it in adultery.

Blister – amber – silver – oranges – apples – sugarstick – hair – spongecake – ivy – roses – ribbon.

The blister reminds her of the burning of her hand as a girl. She sees her own amber hair and her mother's silver hair. This silver is the crown of age but also the stigma of care and grief which she and her lover have laid upon it. This avenue of thought is shunned completely; and the other aspect, amber turned to silver by the years, her mother a prophecy of what she may one day be is hardly glanced at. Oranges, apples, sugarstick – these take the place of the shunned thoughts and are herself as she was, being her girlish joys. Hair: the mind turning again to this without adverting to its colour, adverting only to a distinctive sexual mark and to its growth and mystery rather than to its mystery. The softly growing symbol of her girlhood. Spongecake; a weak flash again of joys which now begin to seem more those of a child than those of a girl. Ivy and roses: she gathered ivy often when out in the evening with girls. Roses grew then a sudden scarlet note in the memory which may be a dim suggestion of the roses of the body. The ivy and the roses carry on and up, out of the idea of growth, through a creeping vegetable life into ardent perfumed flower life the symbol of mysteriously growing girlhood, her hair. Ribbon for her hair. Its fitting ornament for the eyes of others, and lastly for his eyes. Girl-hood becomes virginity and puts on 'the snood that is the sign of maidenhood'. A proud and shy instinct turns her mind away from the loosening of her bound-up hair – however sweet or longed for or inevitable – and she embraces that which is hers alone and not hers and his also – happy distant dancing days, distant, gone forever, dead, or killed?

ROBERT: You have made her all that she is. A strange and wonderful personality.
RICHARD, *darkly*: Or I have killed her.
ROBERT: Killed her?
RICHARD: The virginity of her soul.

Richard must not appear as a champion of woman's rights. His language at times must be nearer to that of Schopenhauer against women and he must show at times a deep contempt for the long-haired, short-legged sex. He is in fact fighting for his own hand, for his own emotional dignity and liberation in which Bertha, no less and no more than Beatrice or any other woman is coinvolved. He does not use the language of ador-ation and his character must seem a little unloving. But it is a fact that for nearly two thousand years the women of Christendom have prayed to and kissed the naked image of one who had neither wife nor mistress nor sister and would scarcely have been associated with his mother had it not been that the Italian church discovered, with its infallible practical instinct, the rich possibilities of the figure of the Madonna.

Snow:
    frost, moon, pictures, holly and ivy, currant-cake, lemonade, Emily Lyons, piano, window sill,

tears:

> ship, sunshine, garden, sadness, pinafore, buttoned boots,
> bread and butter, a big fire.

In the first the flow of ideas is tardy. It is Christmas in Galway, a moonlit Christmas eve with snow. She is carrying picture almanacs to her grandmother's house to be ornamented with holly and ivy. The evenings are spent in the house of a friend where they give her lemonade. Lemonade and currant cake are also her grandmother's Christmas fare for her. She thumps the piano and sits with her dark-complexioned gipsy-looking girl friend Emily Lyons on the window sill.

In the second the ideas are more rapid. It is the quay of Galway harbour on a bright morning. The emigrant ship is going away and Emily, her dark friend, stands on deck going out to America. They kiss and cry bitterly. But she believes that some day her friend will come back as she promises. She cries for the pain of separation and for the dangers of the sea that threaten the girl who is going away. The girl is older than she and has no lover. She too has no lover. Her sadness is brief. She is alone, friendless in her grandmother's garden and can see the garden, lonely now, in which the day before she played with her friend. Her grandmother consoles her, gives her a new clean pinafore to wear and buttoned boots, a present from her uncle, and nice bread and butter to eat and a big fire to sit down to.

Homesickness and regret for dead girlish days are again strongly marked. A persistent and delicate sensuality (visual: pictures, adorned with holly and ivy; gustatious: currant cake, bread and butter, lemonade; tactual: sunshine in the garden, a big fire, the kisses of her friend and grandmother) runs through both series of images. A persistent and delicate vanity also, even in her grief; her pinafore and buttoned boots. No thought of a more recent admiration, which is strong even to the point of being fetichism and has been well observed by her, crosses her mind now. The boots suggest their giver, her uncle, and she feels vaguely the forgotten cares and affection among [which] she grew up. She thinks of them kindly, not because they were kind to her but because

154

they were kind to her girlself which is gone and because they are part of it, hidden away even from herself in her memory. The note of regret is ever present and finds utterance at last in the tears which fill her eyes as she sees her friend go. A departure. A friend, her own youth, going away. A faint glimmer of lesbianism irradiates this mind. This girl too is dark, even like a gipsy, and she too, like the dark lover who sleeps in Rahoon, is going away from her, the man-killer and perhaps also the love-killer, over the dark sea which is distance, the extinction of interest and death. They have no male lovers and are moved vaguely one towards the other, the friend is older, stronger, can travel alone, braver, a prophecy of a later dark male. The passiveness of her character to all that is not vital to its existence, and yet a passiveness which is suffused with tenderness. The assassin is alone and quiet amid the mild sunlight and the mild cares and ministrations of her grandmother, happy that the fire is warm, toasting her toes.

What then is this tenderness and regard to give which is death, or discontent, or distance or the extinction of interest? She has no remorse for she [knows] what she can give when she reads desire in dark eyes. Have they not need of it since they long and ask? To refuse it, her heart tells her, would be to kill more cruelly and pitilessly those whom the waves or a disease or the passing of the years will bear surely away from her life towards distance, early death and that extinction of personality which is death in life.

In the incertitude of the two female characters Bertha has the advantage of her beauty – a fact behind which even an evil woman's character can safely hide much less a character not morally evil.

Act II.
Bertha wishes for the spiritual union of Richard and Robert and *believes* (?) that union will be affected only through her body, and perpetuated thereby.

Richard accepts Robert's homage for Bertha as by so doing he robs it from Bertha's countrywomen and revenges himself and his forbidden love upon them.

The play is three cat and mouse acts.

The bodily possession of Bertha by Robert, repeated often, would certainly bring into almost carnal contact the two men. Do they desire this? To be united, that is carnally through the person and body of Bertha as they cannot, without dissatisfaction and degradation – be united carnally man to man as man to woman?

Exiles – also because at the end either Robert or Richard must go into exile. Perhaps the new Ireland cannot contain both. Robert will go. But her thoughts will they follow him into exile as those of her sister-in-love Isolde follow Tristan?

All believe that Bertha is Robert's mistress. The *belief* rubs against his own *knowledge* of what has been, but he accepts the belief as a bitter food.

Of Richard's friends Robert is the only one who has entered Richard's mind through the gate of Bertha's affection.

The play, a rough and tumble between the Marquis de Sade and Freiherr v. Sacher Masoch. Had not Robert better give Bertha a little bite when they kiss? Richard's Masochism needs no example.

In the last act (or second) Robert can also suggest that he knew from the first that Richard was aware of his conduct and that he himself was being watched and that he persisted because he had to and because he wished to see to what length Richard's silent forbearance would go.

Bertha is reluctant to give the hospitality of her womb to Robert's seed. For this reason she would like more a child of his by another woman than a child of him by her. Is this true? For him the question of child or no child is immaterial. Is her reluctance to yield even when the possibility of a child is removed this same reluctance or a survival of it or a survival of the fears (purely physical) of a virgin? It is certain that her instinct can distinguish between concessions and for her the supreme concession is what the fathers of the church call *emissio seminis inter vas naturale*. As for the accomplishment of the act otherwise externally, by friction, or in the mouth, the question needs to be scrutinized still more. Would she allow her lust to carry her so far as to receive his emission of seed in any other opening of the body where it could not be acted upon, when once emitted, by the forces of her secret flesh?

Bertha is fatigued and repelled by the restless curious energy of Richard's mind and her fatigue is soothed by Robert's placid politeness.

Her mind is a grey seamist amid which common objects – hillsides, the masts of ships, and barren islands – loom with strange and yet recognizable outlines.

The sadism in Robert's character – his wish to inflict cruelty as a necessary part of sensual pleasure – is apparent only or chiefly in his dealings with women towards whom he is unceasingly attractive because unceasingly aggressive. Towards men, however, he is meek and humble of heart.

Europe is weary even of the Scandinavian women (Hedda Gabler, Rebecca Rosmer, Asta Allmers) whom the poetic genius of Ibsen created when the Slav heroines of Dostoievsky and Turgenev were growing stale. On what woman will the light of the poet's mind now shine? Perhaps at last on the Celt. Vain question. Curl the hair how you will and undo it again as you will.

Richard, unfitted for adulterous intercourse with the wives of his friends because it would involve a great deal of pretence on his part rather than because he is convinced of any dishonourableness in it wishes, it seems, to feel the thrill of adultery vicariously and to possess a bound woman Bertha through the organ of his friend.

Bertha at the highest pitch of excitement in Act III enforces her speech with the word 'Heavens'.

The doubt which clouds the end of the play must be conveyed to the audience not only through Richard's questions to both but also from the dialogue between Robert and Bertha.

All Celtic philosophers seemed to have inclined towards incertitude or scepticism – Hume, Berkeley, Balfour, Bergson.

The dialogue notes prepared are altogether too diffuse. They must be sifted in the sieve of the action. Possibly the best way to do this is to draft off the next act (II) letting the characters express themselves. It is not necessary to bind them to the expressions in the notes.

The greatest danger in the writing of this play is tenderness of speech or of mood. In Richard's case it does not persuade and in the case of the other two it is equivocal.

During the second act as Beatrice is not on the stage, her figure must appear before the audience through the thoughts or speech of the others. This is by no means easy.

The character of Archie in the third act carries on the lightheartedness of Richard, which has been apparent at intervals in the first and second acts. However, as Richard's spiritual affection for his son (also his filial feelings towards his own father) has been adequately represented in the former acts to balance this, the love of Bertha for her child must be brought out as strongly and as simply and as early as possible in the third act. It must, of course, be accentuated by the position of sadness in which she finds herself.

Perhaps it would be well to make a separate sketch of the doings of each of the four chief persons during the night, including those whose actions are not revealed to the public in the dialogue, namely Beatrice and Richard.

Robert is glad to have in Richard a personality to whom he can pay the tribute of complete admiration, that is to say, one to whom it is not necessary to give always a qualified and half-hearted praise. This he mistakes for reverence.

A striking instance of the changed point of view of literature towards this subject is Paul de Kock – a descendant surely of Rabelais, Molière and the old *Souche Gauloise*. Yet compare *George Dandin* or *Le Cocu Imaginaire* of Molière with *Le Cocu* of the later writer. Salacity, humour, indecency, liveliness were certainly not wanting in the writer yet he produces a long, hesitating, painful story – written also in the first person. Evidently that spring is broken somewhere.

The relations between Mrs O'Shea and Parnell are not of vital significance for Ireland – first, because Parnell was tongue-tied and secondly because she was an Englishwoman. The very points in his character which could have been of interest have been passed over in silence. Her manner of writing is not Irish – nay, her manner of loving is not Irish. The character of O'Shea is much more typical of Ireland. The two greatest Irishmen of modern times – Swift and Parnell – broke their lives over women. And it was the adulterous wife of the King of Leinster who brought the first Saxon to the Irish coast.